What Others Are Saying About *Pure Praise*

Dwayne Moore's *Pure Praise* gets at the heart of true biblical worship. If you're looking to grow your worship ministry team in its understanding and desire to worship our Creator in spirit and in truth, this book is for you. The weekly studies are practical, insightful, and full of biblical wisdom aimed at getting the reader to grasp how our Creator designed us to worship. This book is a must read for any worship ministry team, and I am glad to recommend it!

Rick Muchow, pastor of worship
Saddleback Church, Lake Forest, California

Dwayne Moore has hit a home run in providing a resource any size church can use to help move to the next level in worship of our most worthy God. I can't wait to see how our Lord will use this life-changing study in the months and years to come!

Charles Billingsley, worship pastor and artist-in-residence
Thomas Road Baptist Church, Lynchburg, Virginia

Dwayne Moore has a writing style that makes you feel like he's right there with you, walking you through each devotional. *Pure Praise* is highly relational and delivered in a way that will minister to you in your personal worship journey as well as find its way into your worship training resource library. This book will help you understand not only the meaning of worship, but also provide you with real tools for leading and ministering in your role as the worship leader.

Julie Reid, executive editor
Worship Leader Magazine

Pure Praise is quite impressive and balanced. It's full of rich biblical content. I've already recommended this study to the praise teams at our church!

Bruce Everhart, manager of marketing and development
Moody Radio

This book will challenge and bless you, your choir, and your congregation. *Pure Praise* is well written, thought-provoking, and well worth your time.

Ray Jones, worship leader
Community Bible Church, San Antonio, Texas

Everyone has opinions about how we should praise, but Dwayne doesn't give his opinions. He pulls incredible principles straight and only from God's Word. I predict this book will influence worshippers and worship leaders for many generations to come.

Dr. Scott Dawson
Evangelist and author of The Complete Evangelism Guidebook

Pure Praise is a comprehensive guide to worship leading. Thorough and well researched, no stone is left unturned. The various application questions and exercises make the book accessible and practical. I highly recommend this book!

Rory Noland
Author of The Heart of the Artist *and* The Worshiping Artist

Seasoned teacher and worship leader Dwayne Moore has created a wonderful and useful tool for both leaders and everyday worshippers alike. What a great resource for your small group, choir, or worship team!

David M. Edwards
Author, songwriter, and editor of The Worshiper *magazine*

Pure Praise is an incredible resource. The book is a valuable tool for teaching and practicing worship. Great organization. Timeless application. Effective teaching concept: nine weeks living the life of praise with Jehoshaphat, learning the joy of seeing God follow through on his promise to honor those who praise him. As my students at the Center for Worship integrate the principles in this book into their daily habit of worship, I'm sure they, too, will learn that when they honor and exalt God, they will experience *Pure Praise* firsthand.

Dr. Vernon M. Whaley
Director, The Center for Worship, Liberty University

This book is amazing! Our entire church experienced revival as our choir went through *Pure Praise*. In fact, we had people joining the choir just so they could go through the study!

Rick Gates, minister through worship
Bowie, Texas

Pure Praise is a study that will enhance worship in your church and your personal walk with Jesus. It is anchored to the Scriptures and leads to encounters with the Holy Spirit. I encourage you to use it.

Dr. Ted Traylor, pastor
Olive Baptist Church, Pensacola, Florida

Not since I first read *Experiencing God* have I been as excited about a new study! Dwayne leads us to understand the *why* and not just the *how* of worship. In a day when too much emphasis is placed upon the performance rather than the heart of the worshipper, this work is refreshing. I highly recommend it!

Phil Waldrep, author and evangelist
Decatur, Alabama

Filled with Scripture references and constantly pointing readers to the Bible, this study will give participants a good foundation and big-picture view of worship from which to live, minister, and study further. Those who go through this study should emerge with a God-exalting understanding of not just worship, but of their responsibilities as both church members and worship team members.

Josh Riley, director
Worship.com

Pure Praise transformed our choir and helped bring revival to our entire church.

Dr. Clay Hallmark, pastor
First Baptist Church, Marion, Arkansas

PURE PRAISE

A Heart-Focused Bible Study on Worship

DWAYNE MOORE

Group

Incredible things will happen™

Loveland, Colorado
group.com

Group resources actually work!

This Group resource incorporates our R.E.A.L. approach to ministry. It reinforces a growing friendship with Jesus, encourages long-term learning, and results in life transformation, because it's

Relational
Learner-to-learner interaction enhances learning and builds Christian friendships.

Experiential
What learners experience through discussion and action sticks with them up to 9 times longer than what they simply hear or read.

Applicable
The aim of Christian education is to equip learners to be both hearers and doers of God's Word.

Learner-based
Learners understand and retain more when the learning process takes into consideration how they learn best.

Pure Praise
A Heart-Focused Bible Study on Worship

Copyright © 2009 Dwayne Moore

Visit our website: **group.com**

Published in association with the literary agency of Sanford Communications, Inc., Portland, Oregon. www.sanfordci.com

Unless otherwise noted, Scripture taken from the HOLY BIBLE, NEW INERNATIONAL VERSION®. Copyright © 1973, 1978, 1984 by International Bible Society. Used by permission of Zondervan Publishing House. All rights reserved.

Quotations in Week 3 taken from *Through the Gates of Splendor* copyright © 1956, 1957, 1981, 1996 by Elisabeth Elliot. Used by permission of Tyndale House Publishers, Inc. All rights reserved. Quotations in Week 4 taken from *The Practice of the Presence of God* copyright © 1982 by Brother Lawrence. Used by permission of Whitaker House, www.whitakerhouse.com. All rights reserved.

Credits

Senior Editor: Candace McMahan
Chief Creative Officer: Joani Schultz
Copy Editor: Janis Sampson
Art Director: Jeff A. Storm

Print Production Artist: Bob Bubnis/Booksetters
Cover Art Director/Designer: Jeff A. Storm
Production Manager: DeAnne Lear
Project Manager: Pam Clifford

Library of Congress Cataloging-in-Publication Data
Moore, Dwayne.
Pure praise : a heart-focused Bible study on worship / Dwayne Moore.
—1st American pbk. ed.
     p. cm.
  ISBN 978-0-7644-3748-9 (pbk. : alk. paper)
   1. Worship—Biblical teaching. I. Title.
BS680.W78M66 2009
248.3—dc22
                        2008024344

10 9 8 7   18 17 16 15 14 13 12 11

C●NTENTS

FOREWORD

Worship is a lifestyle. It should encompass every avenue, attitude, and affection of our lives. It is meant for Monday just as much as Sunday. It is, quite simply, the one element of our lives that should drive all others.

I once heard Louis Giglio give this definition of worship: "Worship is setting your mind's attention and your heart's affection on the Lord…praising him for who he is and what he's done." I have always liked that definition, but I added one phrase to the end: "all the time." Worship is for all the time, everywhere we go, and everything we are a part of.

I am privileged to lead worship for thousands of church members and students each week at Thomas Road Baptist Church and Liberty University, and I see firsthand the tremendous impact worship gatherings can make in a corporate setting. Lives are changed, homes are mended, and God is magnified as his people come together to adore him and give the glory that is due to him.

Yet for all the good that happens in our corporate worship gatherings, it seems many are content to live off of the rich experience of Sunday morning, trying to make it last throughout the entire week. Unfortunately, this is one reason so many corporate worship services lack power, urgency, and fire. We have people filling the pews, but those people are empty on the inside. I believe this is largely because there is a misunderstanding among churchgoers over what worship really is. Yes, it is meant to take place when we join together, but it is also meant to happen when we come humbly before God as individuals.

I am convinced that what makes corporate worship most powerful is the gathering of Christians who have spent time with Jesus all week and who have learned what it means to have the "mind of Christ." It is those Christians who have discovered the source for exuberant praise, and I can read it in their faces every time we gather corporately. We just can't stay close to the Lord worshipping once a week in a crowd. We must worship as individuals!

In individual worship we experience even deeper moments of intimacy with the Savior. In those quiet moments—wrapped in the arms of the One and

Only—we are able to hear the still, small voice of his Spirit. And it is in those moments of solitude that we gather strength from the Mighty One even in our weakest hours. But individual worship is where we are usually weakest. It is easy to come to church. It is quite different to discipline ourselves to enter our closet of prayer each day.

That is why I believe *Pure Praise* is such a vitally needed resource for church members, worship leaders, praise teams, choirs, orchestras, and bands. It is simple to use, yet powerful and effective. It causes us to be awed by God himself—apart from the music and lights and the personalities of corporate worship. It will challenge you and give you a better understanding of Scripture as it relates to you and your life as an individual worshipper.

I have known Dwayne Moore for many years and have always appreciated his passion for worshipping and for leading others in worship. In this book, he has quite effectively used his years of experience and observation to masterfully weave simple-to-understand, yet thought-provoking illustrations into practical worship principles for daily living. It is full of fresh insights and road-weary wisdom from one who has proven the truth of these teachings in his own life and ministry.

Dwayne Moore understands that powerful corporate worship is, in many ways, the overflow of intense individual worship. This book will deepen your individual worship, and in turn, change the way you approach corporate worship. I commend this study to you without reservation.

Charles Billingsley
Worship Pastor, Thomas Road Baptist Church
Artist-in-Residence, Liberty University
www.charlesbillingsley.com

AN INVITATION TO ADVENTURE

Please join me on a journey straight up a tall mountain of learning! Every step we take will move us closer to making our praise to our awesome God more effective and pure. Along the trail we'll discover hidden treasures that are just waiting to be uncovered in the rich soil of God's Word. We'll discover nuggets of truth about our personal praise. We'll unearth ancient artifacts of wisdom about worshipping with other believers. And we'll find lots of precious stones in the form of practical ways to better lead others in praise.

During each of the next nine weeks, you will need to set aside 20 to 30 minutes a day five days a week. You might think of our time each day as a "devotional study." While we'll be learning much head knowledge, it's our *hearts* that must gain the understanding to apply what we're discovering—and be willing to change. Therefore, each day we will have both a study time for our minds and a response time from our hearts.

This book is not meant to be read by itself. It's vitally important that you read from your Bible during each day's lesson. When you see this icon , that's your prompt to read Scripture or pray. Also, please try not to read more than one lesson per day. Your mind and heart need time to meditate on and absorb the truths from each reading. Space is provided to journal your thoughts and responses at the end of each lesson. This is a great way to help solidify and organize what you discover each day.

A Challenge to Climb

This study adventure is not a casual stroll up a hillside. Many who are spiritually faint of heart have craned their necks from a distance and admired those beautiful peaks of praise, wondering what it would be like way up there. But they've never ventured past their comfort zones. Perhaps some teachings and activities surrounding praise and worship have bordered on the weird or sensational. But true biblical worship isn't just for those who live life "on the edge." The kind of worship the Father seeks is as natural as breathing. Worship should only appear strange to people who don't know our God.

Our goal during these weeks is to learn what God says pleases *him* about our worship. After all, he's the one we're praising; therefore, his opinion is the only one that really matters!

For those of us who bear the awesome responsibility of leading others in praise, we really have no choice. We can no longer be content with where we are now or with what we know. As Paul urges us in 2 Timothy 2:15, we must do our best to present ourselves to God "as one approved, a workman who does not need to be ashamed and who correctly handles the word of truth."

Whatever our understanding of worship and praise may be, there will always be more biblical wisdom to discover. Perhaps you're like many who have ignored this mountain of understanding. Or maybe you're like me; you've been gazing up at it, wondering what it would be like to have a view from the top.

Well, wonder no more! Come on, let's put on our hiking boots and head heart-first right up the side of this massive mountain. Let's discover how to worship and praise our great God with all that is in us.

A SPECIAL NOTE TO WORSHIP LEADERS

While the material in this study applies to any believer and can be used as a small group study within the entire church, it works especially well with worship teams, arts teams, choirs, and production crews. This book was designed to help all your praise leaders and ministry volunteers gain a well-rounded understanding of worship and praise and to teach them proven ways to lead praise more effectively.

I can think of no better way to help them grow in these areas than to challenge them to a daily time of Bible study and personal worship. *Pure Praise* is the tool that can lead your group to encounter and experience God through his Word. Each member of your group will need to have his or her own copy of this book in order to do the daily lessons.

For this study to be most effective, a weekly group time is very important. You'll need to set aside 15 to 20 minutes each week with your entire group for nine consecutive weeks. The group times will encourage your people and help hold them accountable to do the daily personal studies. The group times will also foster closeness and unity within your group. I strongly recommend that you do these group times *during* your regular weekly rehearsals if at all possible so you can include and impact the most people.

Wait! Before you put this book down and say, "I can't afford to give up that much time from my rehearsals," consider this: Imagine your entire music ministry group growing together in its understanding and approach to praise and worship. Too often we leaders get frustrated and impatient with the spiritual and biblical shallowness of our people, when, in fact, we are encouraging that shallowness because we don't invest time to *teach* them. Remember, if they know this study is a priority for you, it will become a priority for them.

Before you begin, help your senior pastor understand the importance of these weeks. Work together to plan services that will not tax your musicians as much. For example, during the nine weeks of the study, you might plan to use more familiar music that takes less time to rehearse or perhaps rely more on individuals, rather than on your choir or praise teams, to provide special songs.

Each week, utilize the brief group sessions beginning on page 165. Designed to help participants experience the theme of each week's study, they require no preparation but will go a long way toward cementing important truths in the hearts and minds of the participants.

Commit to this study for your own personal growth. Your teachable spirit and commitment to growth will inspire your people more than anything else you can do.

To augment the study, visit www.NextLevelWorship.com for resources such as DVDs, podcasts, promotional materials, teaching resources, and community forums.

I pray that, through *Pure Praise*, our worthy and wonderful God refreshes you and renews your passion for leading his praises!

Your fellow servant,
Dwayne Moore

THE MEANING

Day 1: Worship Is a Way of Life

I vividly remember the moment I first realized the awesome power of praise. It was both amazing and life changing.

My journey of faith began at the tender age of 6 when I trusted Christ as my Savior. During those early years, God used many Christ-like teachers and mentors to help shape my understanding of him and encourage my Christian walk. However, it wasn't until college that I met someone who challenged my view of praise. His name was Marty. He was known across the campus as a guy who passionately loved Jesus—his walk consistently matched his talk.

One day during my freshman year, Marty invited me to gather with a few friends for some praise time. As he played and sang one song after another, something started to happen. Everyone's focus turned away from Marty and toward our King. Some songs were familiar to me, and some were not. But they all contained thoughts my heart wanted and needed to say to God. Some of the songs were taken straight from Scripture. I felt as though we were actually standing in God's throne room telling him how awesome he is.

You may have experienced this sort of thing many times. If so, count yourself extremely blessed. But I had never seen someone flow for 30 to 40 straight minutes from one song to the next in nonstop, vertical praise. That day—that holy moment—created in me a thirst to know God more and worship him with "all that is within me" (Psalm 103:1, King James Version).

Our Central Passage

Second Chronicles 20 tells a story about hundreds of thousands of people who all had their "light bulb" moment at the same time! Three large armies were marching against Jehoshaphat and the people of Judah. Jehoshaphat's response was to call everyone in Judah to a giant prayer meeting. Every week of this nine-week study, we will draw from a different element of this amazing narrative.

Before you begin, take a moment to ask God to open your spiritual eyes to what he has for you in this passage during the next nine weeks. Then read 2 Chronicles 20:1-30. Try imagining yourself in these scenes.

I'm quite certain I wouldn't have responded the way the people of Judah did when they learned of their imminent danger. Simply put, they made the choice to *worship*.

What we have here is an incredible worship service. In the midst of naturally frightening circumstances, they had a *super*natural encounter with almighty God. They saw him as he is and therefore worshipped him as they should. In fact, they fell down and worshipped him. According to Strong's Concordance, the word *worship* here means "to bow down, prostrate oneself, before a superior in homage, before God in worship." God is our superior; he is our Lord. Submitting to him as our master is the essence of worship.

We are to love the Lord, our God, with everything we are: heart, soul, mind, and body (Deuteronomy 6:4-5). When we do this, we are paying homage to him as our superior. Just as the people of Judah bowed in surrender, we must surrender to him as our Lord. Anything less is not biblical worship.

Jesus verified the priority of worship when he quoted from Deuteronomy 6:4-5. When he was asked, "Of all the commandments, which is the most important?" Jesus replied, "The most important commandment is this: 'Hear, O Israel! The Lord our God is the one and only Lord. And you must love the Lord your God with all your heart, all your soul, all your mind, and all your strength" (Mark 12:28-30, New Living Translation).

People have asked me, "Isn't the Christian life really just a bunch of 'Thou shalt nots'?" To which I reply, "No, the Christian life is actually one big 'Thou shalt'...love God." It's really that simple: *Worship* him completely.

Worship is not just something we do on Sundays at church. And it's certainly more than singing or attending a service, although those are included. Worship is a lifestyle. It involves everything we do and think and are. It means loving God with every breath we take and every move we make. I love how Rick Warren sums it up. Worship, he says, is simply "bringing pleasure to God."[1]

In 1 Corinthians 10:31 Paul wrote, "Whether you eat or drink or whatever you do, do it all for the glory of God." Paul chose the examples of eating and drinking to illustrate how our most common and everyday activities can and should bring glory and honor to Christ.

So what does this kind of worship look like in everyday life? Is it really possible to worship God when you're at home or school or work? How can even your simplest and most common tasks bring honor and worship to God?

Please spend a few minutes considering how you would answer these questions, and write your thoughts in the space below.

In the coming days, we will be "exercising" our praise before God in potentially new and exciting ways. Before a person exercises, it's always a good idea to warm up a bit. As the children of Judah heard Jehoshaphat describing God's faithfulness to them in the past and his promises to them for their future, no doubt their hearts started to "warm up" to praise.

Let's stretch our souls right now. How has God recently shown himself as gracious, merciful, or powerful in your life? Thank him for how faithful he has been. In the space below, write some things about God that you find especially heartwarming at this moment.

JOURNAL }

Ask God to reveal any of your actions or attitudes that are not honoring to him. Write them down; then ask the Lord to forgive you and help you worship him in everything you do today.

JOURNAL }

Day 2: Created for His Praise

Yesterday we discovered that worship is a lifestyle. Everything in our lives— driving a car, mowing grass, doing schoolwork, even eating a cheeseburger— can qualify as pleasing acts of worship. But have you stopped to think why God is interested in even our most menial tasks?

My wife, Sonia, and I have been blessed with two vivacious boys that are three years apart in age. While there's no danger of them ever being called little angels, we do know that they are on loan from God. I am convinced that being a dad is the best calling on earth! Those boys can almost always make me smile, no matter what they're doing. I enjoy watching them play with their GI Joes and

Rescue Heroes. I love to hear them laughing as they watch their favorite cartoon or play in the dirt. Sometimes I stand in their rooms late at night just to watch them sleep.

These guys don't have to be *doing* something in order to please me. They bring me joy and pleasure simply because of who they *are*: my *sons*.

Do you remember what God said when he finished creating man and woman on the sixth day? He said it was "very good" (Genesis 1:31). Think about that. They had not even had the chance to *do* anything, yet he was pleased with them. He enjoyed their company as he walked in the cool of the day with them. They were made in his image; they were a reflection of him. They brought him glory. As God's children we bring him glory, too. Like Adam and Eve, we are created to praise him with our lives.

Read Ephesians 1:3-14. As you read, did you notice that Paul keeps repeating this awesome theme: "to the praise of his glory"? Paul wanted us to see the purpose for our being created. All God has done for us and in us is "to the praise of his glorious grace." Amazing as it may sound, because he loves us he has raised us up and seated us with Christ in heavenly realms so we can one day be trophies of his grace.

H.A. Ironside believed that one of these days we are going to have a part in a great exhibition. From every part of the earth there will be gathered together all who have been redeemed. As Dr. Ironside explains it, the Lord will then show "to all created intelligences how it has been the delight of His heart to show great grace to great sinners. That is our future—a future that does not depend on our faithfulness but on His, who saved us by grace in order that we might show His glories forevermore."[2]

Not only will we be his trophies in the coming ages, we are his witnesses now as living *proof* of his goodness and mercy. First Peter 2:9 states, "You are a chosen people. You are royal priests, a holy nation, God's very own possession. As a result, you can show others the goodness of God, for he called you out of the darkness into his wonderful light" (NLT). In the Old Testament, God chose Israel to represent him to the nations. God called Israel his witnesses (Isaiah 43:10). He said, "I created him [Israel] for my glory" (Isaiah 43:7, KJV). It's no wonder Jehoshaphat, in his prayer in 2 Chronicles 20, reminded God of his dealings with the Jews in the past. God had always displayed his might and willingness to protect and provide for his people.

Second Chronicles 20:29 clearly states that the nations feared the *Lord*, rather than the children of Judah. It was the *Lord* who won the battle. He alone prompted those enemy armies to turn on each other. The people of Judah did nothing but obediently "stand still and see the salvation of the Lord" (verse 17, New King James Version). Once again God worked through his people to bring glory and praise to himself.

And so it should be in every aspect of *our* lives. The fact that we are even living and breathing is a testament of his grace and goodness. No wonder the people of Judah shouted, "Praise the Lord, for his mercy endures forever" (2 Chronicles 20:21, NKJV). May our lives shout it so loud this world can't help but take notice!

My Daily Praise

Meditate on Ephesians 1:3-14 for a few moments. Take the time necessary to let the truths of this passage soak into your soul: Your life has indescribable and unfathomable purpose both now and for eternity. Oh, the love and grace of our Lord! Why not throw yourself your own private praise party to the Lord right now? (Just try to spill a little of that praise over onto this page. You may want to look back to this moment later.)

JOURNAL }

My Daily Surrender

Please read Romans 12:1-2. In view of God's mercy, Paul tells us that our spiritual act of worship is to lay ourselves down on an altar of surrender. God wants our hearts yielded to him, pure and simple. That's what is acceptable to God: giving up control and allowing him to do whatever he wants to do in us and through us. The King James Version calls presenting our bodies as a living sacrifice to him a "reasonable service." As we lay our lives down for him to fill and to use, we become expressions of praise to him. And, considering we were *designed* to bring him glory, such an act is very "reasonable." Write a prayer of surrender right now.

JOURNAL }

Day 3: Worship in All Directions

At some point in your life, you may have been as I was (and so many in our pews still are!). Anytime you heard the word *worship,* you assumed that word mostly referred to singing, clapping, and talking to God. This week we have already seen that worship is actually much more than that: True biblical worship encompasses our entire lives. In fact, in his book *The Ultimate Priority,* John MacArthur Jr. explains that for our worship to be "whole-life" it must include three aspects or *directions.* Most certainly, we worship God when we focus directly on him, pointing our worship *upward* (as we normally think of worship). However, we should also worship God *inwardly.* The third direction we should worship him is *outwardly,* to those around us.[3]

Three Directions of Worship: Inward, Outward, Upward

You might think of three-directional worship like this: Imagine you say to your boss, "You are the greatest boss to ever walk the face of the earth. Furthermore, this is the best job I've ever had or ever will have. In fact, I practically worship at your feet for just letting me do this job every day." (Am I laying it on thick enough yet?) OK, having said such a mouthful *upward* toward your boss, how should you behave when no one's looking? If you really meant what you said, you'll talk well of your boss and your job when your boss isn't around, and you'll work hard and enthusiastically even when no one's watching you. Why? Because *inwardly* you really do love your boss and you want to please him or her.

Now let's take this idea a step further. Let's say you're in the service industry, and your job involves assisting other people. Every time you cheerfully seek to help someone, every time you go out of your way to meet someone's needs, you are *outwardly* honoring your employer and saying by your actions how much you appreciate working for him or her. In much the same way, our God is honored—or worshipped—not only by what we say to him, but also by how much we love him on the inside and by how we respond to those he died for.

Today let's take a closer look at the inward and outward directions of worship. Then tomorrow we'll explore my personal favorite, the upward direction.

The *inward direction* of our worship refers to who I am when no one is looking. It's not really difficult to lift up praises to God when we're at church or around other Christians. In those environments we're encouraged, even expected, to do so. But what about when we're in the privacy of our own homes, browsing the Internet, or glancing though a magazine on the newsstands? Are we being careful to please God with our private thoughts, with the things we see, with the places we visit? (Ouch!)

Worshipping inwardly by being good is perhaps the litmus test for all of worship. If our hearts' desire is to please God, we can no longer enjoy our former sins. Second Corinthians 5:17 says, "If anyone is in Christ, he is a new creation; the old has gone, the new has come!" This refers to a change inside of us. According to Psalm 51:16-17, God wants a broken and contrite heart more than our outward sacrifices. He knows that if our hearts are purely devoted to him, that can't help but affect our outward behavior.

Read Proverbs 4:23. A wellspring is the source from which water flows. Likewise our hearts are the source of all our thoughts, motives, and actions. The importance of this inward direction of worship cannot be overemphasized. As I read 2 Chronicles 16:9, I find that God is searching the earth *not* to support those who sing the best or shout the loudest. Rather, he seeks for those "whose hearts are fully committed to him." As worshippers and worship leaders, that must be our foremost goal. Without that commitment, all other expressions of worship are actually sickening to God (Amos 5:21-23; Psalm 51; Revelation 3:16). (In a moment you will be asked to respond to today's lesson, but if you sense God's leading now, skip to "My Daily Surrender," and write what's on your heart. Please don't put if off, even for a few moments.)

Now let's consider the *outward direction* of worship. There are actually four distinct outward ways we can bring glory to our Lord, and they all have to do with our relationships with other people.

First of all, God is worshipped when we share our faith with someone or in some way play a part in a person's coming to know Christ. In Romans 15:16, Paul says God gave him the "priestly duty of proclaiming the gospel...so that the Gentiles might become an offering acceptable to God." What a privilege to take part in such an offering! Once we've helped someone become eternally transformed, we'll be hooked on sharing our faith for life.

Second, we worship God when we help others. These days, old-fashioned neighborly help can be hard to find. And if we're really honest, most of us are OK with that trend. We often lack the motivation to lend a hand. We build privacy fences so we don't see our neighbors, and then we fill up our schedules so we don't have time to notice if they need our help. But as followers of Jesus, we can't afford not to be the good Samaritans he has called us to be (Luke 10:33). Jesus clearly taught us to give "a cup of cold water" in his name (Matthew 10:42).

Read Philippians 4:14-19. Notice that Paul described the Philippians' gifts as "a fragrant offering, an acceptable sacrifice, pleasing to God" (verse 18). Giving financial aid to those in need is a third wonderful way to express our love for God. However, it's imperative that we be cheerful when we give, not grudging, because that represents the real motives of our hearts (2 Corinthians 9:7). Once again, God considers our willing and compassionate hearts as the source of true worship.

The fourth way we worship God outwardly is by being sensitive to our weaker brothers and sisters. The entirety of Romans 14 focuses on strong and weak Christians. According to verse 13, we are to "live in such a way that you will not cause another believer to stumble and fall" (NLT). Verse 18 shows God's view of this: "If you serve Christ with this attitude, you will please God" (NLT).

For some reason, my father (who was not a Christian) didn't think Christian women should wear shorts. So when I was growing up, I never saw our next-door neighbor wearing shorts. She chose not to wear them in front of my dad because she didn't want to offend him. That's the kind of selfless sensitivity God honors in us—and is honored in.

Because our entire study is based on 2 Chronicles 20, I want to close this lesson by focusing for a moment on Jehoshaphat, that story's main character. The Bible says, "Jehoshaphat was a good king, following the example of his father, Asa. He did what was pleasing in the Lord's sight" (1 Kings 22:43, NLT). He was obviously a man of character, a good man on the *inside*. He also respected his people and taught them the Word of God (2 Chronicles 17:7). He protected them. In fact, he had over a million men ready and

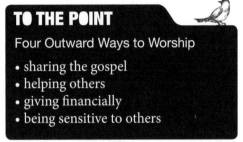

TO THE POINT
Four Outward Ways to Worship
- sharing the gospel
- helping others
- giving financially
- being sensitive to others

willing to fight in his army! No wonder he was "highly esteemed" by the people (2 Chronicles 17:5, NLT). In short, Jehoshaphat not only said he loved and honored God, he exemplified his passion and commitment to God by who he was and how he acted toward others. He was a man who worshipped God with his *whole life*.

My Daily Surrender

Hebrews 4:12 says the Word of God "exposes our innermost thoughts and desires" (NLT). Who are you *really*? Be honest before God right now. Are any of your attitudes or actions offensive to another Christian? Do you cheerfully give your money as you feel led by God? Be honest and open with God as you write your thoughts in the space below.

JOURNAL

Decide today to consciously and deliberately express your worship outwardly. Look for an opportunity to share your faith or give to someone in need. Pray and commit yourself to *whole-life* worship today.

Day 4: Lifting Up Thanksgiving and Praise

As we saw yesterday, worship is three-directional: inward, outward, and upward. Conveniently, Hebrews 13:15-16 touches on all three of these aspects of a worshipping life.

Please read that passage now. Notice that the passage concludes with these words: "for with such sacrifices God is pleased."

The aspect we are focusing on today is the third: worship pointed *upward,* toward God. It's what most folks think of when they hear the word *worship.* In Hebrews 13:15 the upward direction involves two specific actions: praise and thanksgiving: "Let us continually offer the sacrifice of praise to God, that is, the fruit of our lips, giving thanks to His name" (NKJV). Praise is primarily acknowledging God for who he is. Thanksgiving, on the other hand, is giving thanks to God for what he has done for us. Next week we will dedicate ourselves to a better understanding of praise, but today we will focus on the priority of being thankful.

We can be sure nothing ever happens to us that our loving God doesn't permit. After all, like Moses, he protects us "in the cleft of the rock" as he covers us with his mighty hand (Exodus 33:22, NKJV). His rod of correction and his staff of protection and direction should bring us great comfort at all times (Psalm 23:4). But let's be honest here. We know we should be humbly grateful. Yet there are times when we are tempted to be grumbly hateful!

I once heard Dr. Ben Haden share a story during his radio broadcast of a young couple who entered the hospital to have their baby. Complications arose. Tests results showed that their child had Down syndrome. By this time, word had spread throughout the hospital about this young couple and their yet-to-be-born baby.

Word had also gotten around that these parents were Christians. So several nurses and employees began to speculate about how these "God-fearing" people would respond. Many, including the hospital switchboard operator, expected them to become angry at God. However, the couple maintained an upbeat attitude. Not to be proven wrong, the switchboard operator decided to listen in on their private phone conversations. What she heard would change her life forever. Rather than spewing bitterness and doubt toward God, the young mother repeatedly stated her trust and thankfulness in her Lord. She said that no matter what, they knew God would work the situation out for their good and his glory.

Not only did that operator surrender her life to Christ, but as a result of those parents' faith, over 20 nurses and doctors walked the aisle of that couple's church the following Sunday and trusted in Jesus!

Apparently that new mom and dad understood that God would be with them in the midst of unexpected or difficult circumstances. Before any of us can give thanks and praise to the Father and really mean it, we, too, must accept God's sovereignty in our hearts.

There is a throne in heaven. And it is *occupied!* Our great God, mighty and majestic Father, is sitting on that throne right now. This world may seem as if it's spinning out of control, but God is still the all-powerful, all-knowing, ever-present King of kings and Lord of lords—the same God who loves you and me.

Stop right now and thank God for loving and watching over you at this very moment.

Take a look at 1 Thessalonians 5:18. Notice that we are not told to give thanks *for* our circumstances, but rather *in* them. We are not expected to be thankful for problems and hardships that come our way.

However, if we clearly understand that God reigns and that he is using our circumstances to make us more like him and to bring him greater glory, then we can be thankful to him constantly, even while we're going through the tough times. This is sometimes called an attitude of gratitude.

I recently purchased a book for my boys titled *Hermie,* by Max Lucado. It's the story of two caterpillars named Hermie and Wormie. Hermie and Wormie are common caterpillars. So common and uninteresting, in fact, that they don't even have any stripes or spots on them. When they bring their complaints of commonness to God, he reminds them that he is not finished with them yet. He is giving them a new heart, he tells them. This makes them feel better for a while; nonetheless, each time they meet an insect with a unique ability they wish they had, they begin complaining again. (Sound familiar?) Eventually Hermie decides to simply be thankful for how God made him. Not so coincidentally, that same night he turns into a beautiful butterfly! His heart, however, had already been changed.[4]

My Daily Praise

An old song tells us, "Count your many blessings; see what God has done." From time to time, I've found it both humbling and thrilling to make a list of things I'm thankful for: the good, the bad, and the ugly. Take some time now to write down every blessing you can think of. (Remember, blessings can come disguised as heartaches.)

{ JOURNAL

Talk to God about anything in your life for which you're finding it hard to be thankful. Be honest and open with him. He already knows what you're feeling anyway. Ask him to help you be thankful *in* that situation. Ask him to change your heart. Then decide to be thankful throughout your day today, deliberately looking for God's presence in each and every circumstance. Write your prayer in the space below.

JOURNAL }

Day 5: True Worship Changes Us

My wife has the "green thumb" in our family. She loves and cares for her plants. She makes sure they get plenty of everything they need to be healthy and happy (if plants can be happy...). Occasionally she moves a plant closer to a window if she sees that it isn't getting enough sunlight. It always amazes me how quickly the plants perk up and look healthy (and happy) again.

Worshipping God has a similar effect on our souls. We cannot encounter his presence and awesome glory and not somehow be affected.

Returning to the story of Jehoshaphat and the people of Judah, read 2 Chronicles 20:2-4. How do you think you would have felt if you'd received the news of the three approaching armies? According to verse 3, Jehoshaphat was alarmed. That so many people came together to seek the Lord indicates that they were fearful as well.

Now read verses 17-19. Notice the attitude of the people of Judah *after* God spoke through his prophet. What made them go from shaking with fear to shouting with joy? One big wonderful word: *GOD*. God showed up in that place, and their entire outlook changed. The people of Judah were full of fear as they gathered to seek God, but they left full of faith.

In Psalm 73 Asaph undergoes a similar change through worship. Talk about a major attitude adjustment!

Please read Psalm 73:2-14. Notice Asaph's negative outlook in these verses. He was focused on the prosperity of the wicked. Now read verses 18-28. See how his whole focus changed? Rather than remaining so discouraged that he wanted to quit, he now saw the end of the wicked. He now proclaimed, "Earth has nothing I desire besides you" (verse 25). In fact, Asaph suddenly turned all his attention toward God. While he barely mentioned God's name in the first half of this chapter, now Asaph prayed directly to God. What made such a huge difference? I mean, imagine if a psychologist could tap into Asaph's secret. He'd put Dr. Phil out of business! This was pretty potent medicine!

What did Asaph do that totally changed his outlook? Please read the three verses we skipped (verses 15-17). When Asaph entered "the sanctuary of God," he saw the final destiny of the wicked. There he turned his eyes back to the Lord and got a proper perspective of everything around him. Amazing!

Another great example of the transforming power of worship is in Isaiah 6. At the beginning of this chapter, Isaiah was mourning the death of his friend King Uzziah. Through a vision Isaiah found himself right in the middle of a heavenly worship service. He "saw the Lord seated on a throne, high and exalted" (verse 1). He went on to describe the seraphs all calling to one another, "Holy, holy, holy is the Lord God Almighty." Their voices were so loud that the entire place shook. The Temple was filled with smoke, which represented the holy presence of God.

Can you imagine what that service must have been like? Wouldn't you love to have been there with Isaiah? But notice that Isaiah wasn't actually "in" the service at first. Verse 1 says he "saw the Lord." He was an observer, an onlooker. Perhaps he was like some of those who come to our worship services—not really participating, just watching. But even the person in the farthest corner of the room will be somehow affected when God shows up. That's exactly what happened to Isaiah. He couldn't stay uninvolved for long.

Take a look at Isaiah 6:5-8. Isaiah's first response was to recognize his sinfulness. When God's light of perfect holiness shines on us, it always exposes our *un*holiness. In God's presence Isaiah's sin was more than he could bear.

God never points out our sin to condemn us. Rather, he shows us our sin so we, like Isaiah, will acknowledge and turn from it. He "touches our lips" and hearts and forgives us.

Isaiah went from a downcast and reluctant worship spectator to a willing participant in anything God wanted him to do. He didn't even wait to be singled out. He enthusiastically volunteered to go. That's the amazing change God can make in people's lives through worship. Perhaps you've been in a service in "the sanctuary of God" when people started coming to the altar during a powerful moment of worship without any formal invitation from the pastor. If so, no doubt you long to see that kind of outpouring toward God again and again.

My Daily Praise

In Psalm 63:2 David wrote, "I have seen you in the sanctuary and beheld your power and your glory." Perhaps you remember a worship service or a personal quiet time in which, as he did with David, God gave you a glimpse of his glory. How did it affect you, and how were you changed? Now think about a song that expresses your praise and thanksgiving to the Lord. Sing it or speak it to God now.

JOURNAL }

My Daily Surrender

What has God revealed to you that you need to confess or commit to him?

Pray now and ask God to "show up and show off" this weekend during your church's worship services. Ask him to change lives—starting with your own. Use the space below to write your thoughts.

JOURNAL }

1. Rick Warren, *The Purpose-Driven Life* (Grand Rapids, MI: Zondervan, 2002), 64.
2. H.A. Ironside, *Galatians and Ephesians* (Neptune, NJ: Loizeaux Brothers, 1983), 109-110.
3. John MacAruthur Jr., *The Ultimate Priority* (Chicago: Moody Press, 1983), 14-16.
4. Max Lucado, *Hermie* (Nashville, TN: Tommy Nelson, 2002).

Day 1: The Priority of Praise

Have you ever looked out the window of an airplane just before it pierces the clouds and noticed how much of the terrain you could see from that one vantage point? You suddenly begin to realize just how enormous this earth of ours really is.

Today let's imagine we're "flying over" and looking down at this thing called praise. As we take this broad view of praise, we'll begin to notice two things that show us just how important to the Lord praise really is. First, we'll realize that praise, like land and water seen from an airplane, stretches as far as the mind can perceive in all directions. It is infinitely vast. We'll wait to discover the second characteristic that verifies the priority God places on praise. It will become obvious only after we've craned our necks for a while looking out our little "window of understanding."

Speaking of understanding, let's stop now and pray that our eyes will be opened to what our Lord has to teach us today.

Praise Is Prevalent

As we scan the "plains of praise," we see many landmarks that give us a clear picture of how far-reaching praise to God is:

1. God's people have always praised him. I've been a praise leader for a long time. In fact, I was leading worship "when worship wasn't cool." It's exciting now to see just how far praise has come. More and more churches and individual Christians are embracing greater freedom in worship. Praise is no longer just for "that denomination down the street." With strong teaching on biblical worship and praise, this freedom will continue far beyond any worship fad.

In one form or another, praise to our wonderful God has always been in vogue among his followers. In Psalm 33, the opening words of the call to worship include "Sing joyfully to the Lord, you righteous; it is fitting for the upright to praise him." Throughout Israel's history, the people's most shining moments—those most pleasing to God—were times they lifted God up in praise. In fact, David said of God, "You are the praise of Israel" (Psalm 22:3).

We've already seen in 2 Chronicles 20:18 that "all the people of Judah and Jerusalem fell down in worship before the Lord." Some Levites even praised God "with loud voices" (verse 19). Whether they were kneeling quietly or being loud and joyful, they never considered what they were doing as strange or inappropriate. The fact that *all* of Judah bowed in worship shows that praise was not just for the "less educated" or "less cultured." Rather, it was *every* believer's most natural response to God's power and grace.

2. Throughout God's Word we find praise being lifted up to him. The word *praise* can be found well over 200 times in the Bible. When we include related words such as *worship*, *sing*, *shout*, and *bow down*, that number climbs to close to 500.

3. For all eternity God will be praised. Please read Jude 24-25. Stop now and imagine yourself in heaven saying or singing those words to God. How long do you think you will need to fully express your gratitude and adoration to him?

Now please turn in your Bible to Revelation 4. Read the entire chapter carefully. Take time to soak in this amazing scene.

This chapter describes part of a vision John, the author of Revelation, had of a glorious gathering in heaven that will take place at some point in the future. It's interesting to note, however, that everything John described was in the past tense because he was telling about a heavenly vision he had already *seen*. Yet when he spoke of the *praise* taking place in heaven in verses 8 through 11, John suddenly spoke in the here and now. Notice the verbs that are used in these verses: *saying, give, sits, worship, lives, lay, say.*

What do all these words have in common? They are all in the present tense. I believe John's abrupt change from the past tense to the present tense was intentional. John wanted to be clear that the praise he was witnessing was not a one-time event. Praise in heaven is ongoing, both in the present and in the never-ending future!

4. Throughout all creation God will be praised. Read Revelation 5:11-14. All heavenly beings, including angels, living creatures, and elders will praise him. Every created being, including people, animals, fish, and all of nature will sing to him. Praise is obviously both pleasing to God and natural for his creation.

5. At this very moment in heaven, God is being praised. This is perhaps the most amazing of all. Please read Revelation 4:8 again. Did you notice that the four living creatures *never* stop saying, "Holy, holy, holy is the Lord God Almighty"? You may recall that was precisely what they kept saying in Isaiah's vision, too. So if they said those words in the past and they will be saying them in the future, it's reasonable to conclude they must be saying them *now!* Praise to our holy God is so important that heaven itself never stops praising him. I know how easy it is to sometimes feel in the minority during worship services—especially when it seems you're about the only one in the whole congregation who is participating. But be encouraged: There is a loud roar of praise to God in heaven at the *exact* moment you are praising him.

Praise Is Inevitable

OK, imagine we're still sitting by that little window on the plane. So far, we've been impressed with how enormous and vast praise is. But now we've climbed to cruising altitude, and we discover something more.

Imagine yourself looking down from the airplane window *below* those scattered clouds. What's down *there*? Remember, we're taking a bird's-eye view of *praise*. So it's really *praise* you're seeing below us.

So what's down there? The same thing that's been there since we took off—praise. Even if you look away, it's fairly safe to predict that praise will be there the next time you look. You can *count* on it.

Praise is *inevitable*. While God desires praise from his people, he *expects* it from the rest of his creation. David wrote, "The heavens declare the glory of God" (Psalm 19:1, KJV). That means every day of every year of every century, the heavens are proclaiming his greatness and his worth. Do you remember Jesus' words to the Pharisees when they told him to quiet his noisy disciples during the triumphal entry? "I tell you," Jesus replied, "if they keep quiet, the stones will cry out" (Luke 19:40). I'm sure I speak for both of us when I say I don't want any rocks to take my place! But if we don't praise him, they will—because God is going to get the praise he deserves…period.

My Daily Praise

Please read all of Revelation 5. Every time you come to a song in this chapter of Scripture, read it out loud with conviction as though you are right there with the angels. (If you know Christ, you will be in that scene one day. So you might as well get some practice in now!) You may even want to make up a tune to go with those awesome lyrics.

My Daily Surrender

What's been your attitude toward praise in the past? Write your response to what God has shown you today about praising him.

JOURNAL

Day 2: Perfect Praise

Last week we saw that worship to God should include everything we do. Our very breathing in and out is an expression of our worship and a testimony to

God's faithfulness in our lives. We also learned that praise is but one part of worship. Stated another way, while all acceptable praise is worship, not all worship is praise. Praise is that *upward* focus toward God. You may not even consider some of the things you do to be worship because they flow so naturally from your heart and mind and are almost unconsciously given to God. However, you are almost sure to know when you're praising him. That's because praise is direct and deliberate adoration. Praise is a *choice*.

Please read 2 Chronicles 20:18-21. Notice the two references to praise in this passage. In verse 19, "Some Levites…praised the Lord." Jehoshaphat, in verse 21, "appointed men…to praise him." The word translated as "praise" in these verses is the Hebrew word *hallal*. In order for us to appreciate the people of Judah's resolve to praise their God, we need to take a closer look at this word. It is used 99 times in the Old Testament, more than any other major word translated "praise."[1] Together with *Jah* (which is the shortened form of God's name, Yahweh), *hallal* makes up the first two syllables of our most famous praise word, *hallelujah*, which means "Let us praise Yah." The definition of hallal is "to praise, celebrate, glory, sing (praise), boast."[2] Strong's Concordance includes in the definition "to rave." There was nothing accidental or unintentional about their actions toward the Lord that day in Jerusalem. They deliberately and boldly praised him, no matter how mad or foolish it may have seemed.

I was in Salt Lake City a few years ago leading the music for a group of students on their mission trip. Every morning after our worship service, we would go out on buses and vans into the community to share our faith. One day as we were riding to our assigned area, everyone in the bus started singing praise songs. We sang and sang. The girl beside me was one of those Christians who had the "glow that shows." Her smile was contagious. She kept smiling even while she was singing. At the end of one of our songs, she looked up at me and said an amazing thing. She said, "You know, I don't sing very well." She paused for moment, the whole time maintaining that wonderful smile. Then she said, "But that's OK with me, because I figure this: God made my voice. And since he made my voice, he must like to hear it." Now her smile got even bigger and brighter. "So I'm just gonna sing as loud as I can!"

That girl made a *choice* to praise God with her voice. It didn't matter to her if others thought she was "un-cool" or even fanatical. What motivated her to praise was nothing less than passionate love for and devotion to her Lord. Praise can be defined as "the bubbling over of a hot heart." Evidently that young girl had a hot heart for God. Praise was bubbling out of her!

Luke 7:36-50 describes another woman whose praise was motivated by a heart that was boiling over with devotion. She poured a very expensive gift on Jesus. Please read that story in your Bible now. Do you see how this was a deliberate act of praise? The woman outwardly expressed her love to Christ.

Let's look at one more example, a group of children who made the conscious choice to praise their Savior. In Matthew 21:14-16, as Jesus healed the blind and the lame at the Temple, the children cried out, "Hosanna to the Son of David!" When the Pharisees became indignant, Jesus responded, "Have you never read, 'Out of the mouth of babes and nursing infants you have perfected praise'?" (NKJV).

Those children were praising God in much the same way the children of Judah did in 2 Chronicles 20. They were praising, celebrating, singing, and boasting about the Lord—perhaps even looking a bit foolish!

Three Requirements for Perfect Praise

In this passage Jesus teaches us something else about praise. He quoted Psalm 8:2 when he said, "Out of the mouth of babes and nursing infants." He added, "you have perfected praise." What did he mean by that? Did he mean praise isn't perfect on its own? Is it not sufficient to simply throw a party and celebrate and boast about the Lord? Actually, no…We could do everything that the word *praise* implies and still accomplish nothing more than to send up a bunch of *im*perfect noise.

Amos 5:21-23 sheds light on this. Please read that passage now. God calls the worship of those who don't truly seek him "noise." Paul summed it up like this: "Though I speak with the tongues of men and of angels, but have not love, I have become as sounding brass or a clanging symbol" (1 Corinthians 13:1, NKJV). From these passages, we are challenged to search out what God considers *perfect* praise. That is the *only* kind we can be certain God will accept from us.

After his rebuke of the Pharisees in Matthew 21, Jesus lays out three requirements necessary to offering up perfect and acceptable praise to God.

In verse 16, Jesus starts with the words, "Out of the mouth" (NKJV). During his Sermon on the Mount, Jesus had already taught an important insight about our mouths. He said, "The good man brings good things out of the good stored up in his heart…For out of the overflow of his heart, his mouth speaks" (Luke 6:45). He is telling us here that the first requirement for praise to be perfect is this: Perfect praise emerges from a worshipful and passionate heart. God hated to hear the songs of Israel in Amos 5 because their praise did not spring from love for him; their hearts were *evil*. They had committed "manifold transgressions and…mighty sins" (Amos 5:12, NKJV).

Next, in Matthew 21:16, Jesus says, "of babes and nursing infants" (NKJV). The second requirement of perfect praise, then, is that we approach him as little children. This doesn't mean we should act childish. Rather, what God wants to see in us are certain childlike qualities.

For instance, little children are humble (Matthew 18:4). Children are also trusting. I once heard a story of a small boy whose grandfather had promised him a certain red rocking horse for Christmas. His granddad lived across the ocean in a faraway country, so the rocking horse would have to be shipped weeks in advance. Every day the little boy eagerly awaited the rocking horse's arrival. But with Christmas only a few days away, his parents began to tell him that maybe his prized horse wouldn't make it or perhaps his grandfather had forgotten to send it. The little boy kept saying, "No, Granddaddy *promised* it would be here. So it's coming; you'll see." Christmas Eve arrived, and still no rocking horse. Regardless, the little boy's faith in his grandfather was not at all shaken. "I'm getting a rocking horse for Christmas. It will be here in the morning. Granddaddy promised," he insisted.

By now the parents didn't have the heart to tell their son there would be no more shipments before Christmas. Then, early Christmas morning, a loud knock awoke everyone. Standing at the door was none other than Granddaddy himself, and in his arms was that bright red rocking horse, ready to be loved by one very *trusting* little boy! In the same way we must trust the God whom we are praising—regardless of the circumstances.

There is one other childlike quality we must have, and that is total dependence. Little kids, especially infants, are helpless on their own. They must rely on someone else to do everything for them.

That leads us to the third and final aspect of perfect praise. It is summed up in one all-important word: "Out of the mouth of babes and nursing infants, You…" (NKJV). The "You" Jesus was referring to is God himself. "*You* have perfected praise" (italics mine). We must depend on God to initiate and perfect our praise. It was God who put it in the hearts of those little ones to celebrate Jesus in the Temple. The Father was perfectly blessed by their praises because *he* set up that entire praise moment. There was *no* doubt their praise would be accepted by he who matters most—our audience of One.

My Daily Praise

Write a prayer of thanksgiving and praise to God. Thank him for the privilege of praising him. Pour from your heart words of love and adoration. Praise is a choice. Consider praising him now for an attribute of his character, such as his love or omnipresence.

JOURNAL }

It's no wonder the heavens consistently and completely declare God's glory. They're doing exactly what they were *designed* to do! If we want to be sure God is pleased with our praise, we must get ourselves out of the way and pray a prayer like David's: "O Lord, open my lips, and my mouth shall show forth Your praise" (Psalm 51:15, NKJV). Ask God to show you what you need to do today to *perfect* your praise.

{ JOURNAL

Day 3: Ways to Praise

Have you ever thought how strange praise must appear to those who don't know Christ? (After all, why would anyone want to sing and carry on for a God they can't see or touch?) People around you may never know you are worshipping God through the normal activities of your day. But if anyone happens to be nearby when you're compelled to praise, they'll not only notice you, they'll probably wonder what you could possibly be doing.

Say, for example, you're sitting at a red light. Your favorite praise CD is blaring. Before you know it, you're lost in the moment. You start lifting your hands, singing at the top of your lungs. For you this kind of behavior may be perfectly normal. But imagine what the guy beside you must be thinking. He can't hear what you're singing, but what he sees definitely has his attention. He's probably thinking, "Why does that person have her hands up? If she's trying to reach the sun visor, it would help if she opened her eyes!"

Praise, by its very nature, is outward, open, demonstrative, and obvious to anyone watching. We are exhorted numerous times in Psalms to praise the Lord publicly and outwardly: "Let them exalt him also in the congregation of the people, and praise him in the assembly of the elders" (Psalm 107:32, KJV). "I will praise the Lord with my whole heart, in the assembly of the upright, and in the congregation" (Psalm 111:1, KJV).

David writes in Psalm 40:3, "He has given me a new song to sing, a hymn of praise to our God. Many will see what he has done and be amazed. They will put their trust in the Lord" (NLT). Apparently we are not only to praise God among the saints but also in front of those who have never placed their trust in the Lord. We are on this earth to make our God known through our praise. What a privilege! What a responsibility! So we had better know every possible avenue available to us to praise him.

Eight Expressions of Praise

And that brings us to our study of the eight expressions of praise. Jack Taylor, in his groundbreaking classic, *The Hallelujah Factor*, has grouped them into three categories to help us remember them. One category is *vocal* and includes singing and shouting, as well as speaking. The second category is *audible* and includes clapping and playing instruments. A third category does not involve any sounds. That group, called *visible*, includes kneeling, dancing, and raising our hands.[3] Today we'll consider visible expressions of praise.

In the account of the worship service in 2 Chronicles 20:18, the Hebrew word used to describe how the children of Judah responded is *shachaw*. It is often translated "worship," but is also translated in the King James as "bow down," "reverence," "fall down," "stoop," and "crouch." First Chronicles 16:29 says, "Bring an offering and come before him; worship *(shachaw)* the Lord in the splendor of his holiness."

Do you remember what the Magi did when they first saw the baby Jesus? Like the children of Judah, they knelt or stooped as an act of worship (Matthew 2:11). They had to physically bend the knee or somehow crouch down. These are both obvious and deliberate positions of the body. The Greek word for worship as used for what the Magi did is *proskuneo* which literally means "to kiss, like a dog licking his master's hand." It is humbling and powerfully worshipful to bow down before our great Master.

Another way to praise God is through dancing. Read Psalm 149:3. Why do you think David exhorted people to dance as an expression of praise?

I grew up in a denomination that's been somewhat reluctant to embrace this particular form of praise. Like anything else we do, dancing can be done for the wrong motives and in the wrong ways. Nevertheless, genuine, joyful dancing before God and *for* God is absolutely biblical.

Another visible form of praise is raising our hands. We are exhorted in several passages to lift up our hands. One of my favorites is Psalm 63:4: "I will praise you as long as I live, and in your name I will lift up my hands."

Please read Nehemiah 8:5-6. The people responded when Ezra read from the Law by lifting their hands. The Hebrew word used in these verses is *yadah*. *Yadah* is the second most frequently occurring word that is translated "praise" in the Old Testament. It means "to worship with extended hands, to throw out the hands, to give thanks to God." It is often translated "thanks" or "thanksgiving" in the English translations.[4] *Yadah* is the exact word Jehoshaphat used to instruct the singers when he appointed them to go out at the head of the army saying, "Give thanks *(yadah)* to the Lord" (2 Chronicles 20:21b). Now we can add another dimension to our mental picture of this amazing story: Imagine hundreds of musicians leading the army, sing-ing at the top of their lungs with their hands stretched toward the sky.

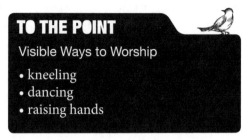

TO THE POINT

Visible Ways to Worship

- kneeling
- dancing
- raising hands

Perhaps you have a son or daughter or grandchild. How did you feel the first time you saw this child looking up at you with those big eyes and holding out those tiny hands? You probably stopped whatever you were doing and reached down to hold that child, didn't you? Imagine how our Father must feel when we reach up for him!

My Daily Praise

Today we begin our "daily exercises" in the eight expressions of praise. Many have never experienced freedom to praise among other Christians because they've never tried certain forms of praise in private. Make sure you're alone and no one is watching. It's just you and God. Now, give this a try…

If you're physically able, kneel where you are before the Lord. Raise both your hands before him. While your hands are lifted, sing one of your favorite praise songs to God, or simply tell him how much you love him.

My Daily Surrender

The Bible is clear that we should lift up "holy hands" to God in prayer, "without anger or disputing" (1 Timothy 2:8). Confess to him any sins you haven't already brought to him. If he doesn't reveal an unconfessed sin to you, thank him for his cleansing, and ask him to help you keep your hands and your heart clean today. Write your response to God in the space below.

JOURNAL

Day 4: Vocal Praise

When I was growing up, my family attended a rather reserved church service every week. You might say our congregation was fairly content with keeping our adventures in praise to a minimum. Weekly singing and an occasional faith story just about summed it up. However, one dear lady managed to rouse us from our lethargy from time to time. Her name was Aunt Bessie. Every fifth Sunday or so, she'd let out a shout that would wake all of us "dignified" folks up! Aunt Bessie loved God passionately and walked closely with him. Whenever she got "happy," the rest of us knew God was up to something in that particular service, so we had better sit up and take notice.

Aunt Bessie was not the first person to shout out in worship. Actually, shouting was quite common among the people of Israel.

Take a look at 1 Samuel 4:5-6. Some of the specific definitions for the word translated *shout* here are "alarm," "signal," "sound of tempest," "battle-cry," and "shout of joy." That same word is used in Ezra 3:10-13. In this passage, the Israelites had only recently returned from exile. Their first Temple had been destroyed years before, and now they were rebuilding it. They sang to the Lord "with praise and thanksgiving." Then they *all* gave a great shout of praise to the Lord. Their shouts and weeping made a noise that was heard far away.

Have you ever been in a football stadium when the home team scored a touchdown? The celebratory shouts are deafening. Wouldn't it be wonderful if, the next time someone comes forward to receive Christ in our churches, we all stood up and shouted, "Touchdown, Jesus!"? Psalm 5:11 says, "Let them ever shout for joy, because You defend them" (NKJV). Shouting isn't just for a few people like Aunt Bessie, but for all of us whom the Lord defends.

The second—and by far the most common—vocal way to praise is singing. There's something about singing that unites us no matter how diverse our backgrounds or cultures may be. One of my greatest joys has been directing music for citywide festivals and crusades. It's like a little heaven on earth to hear Christians from so many different denominations and traditions of worship singing a great praise song such as "Amazing Grace" or "How Great Is Our God."

Isaiah 51:11 tells us, "So the ransomed of the Lord shall return, and come to Zion with singing, with everlasting joy on their heads; They shall obtain joy and gladness, and sorrow and sighing shall flee away" (NKJV). Psalm 100:2 says, "Worship the Lord with gladness. Come before him, singing with joy" (NLT). This verse leaves no doubt about how we should sing to the Lord. The Hebrew word for *sing* in Psalm 100:2 is *renanah*, which literally means "joyful voice," as in joyful, triumphal singing. When we sing God's praise, we should be full of joy. How can any song about God or our salvation be depressing, even if we're having a bad day or week?

Please turn to Isaiah 54:1-3, and read Isaiah's exhortation to Israel. Even the "woman," Jerusalem, who could not bear spiritual children at that time, should sing. And the word for *singing* here again includes the idea of crying out in joy. How can someone going through a trying time still manage to sing with excitement and inner joy? Notice that in the last part of verse 3, the Lord is giving barren Jerusalem words of hope. There's the key: *hope* in God. That's how we can get up week after week and sing and praise with consistent enthusiasm. We *always* have hope!

One more way to praise vocally is to speak to God and also to tell others about what he has done in our lives. Psalm 107:2 says, "Let the redeemed of the Lord say so" (KJV). Once while I was leading a *Pure Praise* conference at a church, I saw

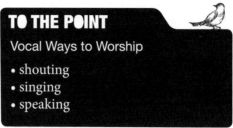

TO THE POINT

Vocal Ways to Worship

• shouting
• singing
• speaking

as never before the impact a faith story can have in a service. We had sung almost all the songs we had planned to sing. We had done about everything in our order of worship. Nonetheless, the service had been dry and apparently uneventful.

We were about to close the service when toward the back of the church one little lady who appeared to be in her 80s slowly stood up. Her words were brief and to the point. She simply wanted everyone to know her Lord had always been faithful to her. One by one, others started standing as well. (Coming back from the dead was more like it!) Each had a unique and emotional story of God's faithfulness. People started flooding to the altar. Forty-five minutes later the service was still going strong. And it all started when one redeemed woman "said so."

My Daily Praise

Continuing with our "daily praise exercises," sing a song to God *out loud* right now. Then look for someone to talk with about the Lord today.

My Daily Surrender

Ask God to help you stay alert today to ways you can vocally express your praise. Commit your way to him. Let him know you'll trust him for the outcome of this day. Write your thoughts in the space below.

JOURNAL

Day 5: Audible Praise

Now we come to our final expression of praise: audible. There are two ways that do not involve our voices but can still be heard. The first is playing an instrument.

Read Psalm 150. Notice there are enough instruments for an orchestra! Brass, wind, stringed, and percussion instruments are included. As far back as Miriam, the people of Israel used instruments to praise God. Miriam took a tambourine in her hand as she danced and sang to the God who had just delivered Israel from Pharaoh's army. (See Exodus 15:20-21.)

There has been a resurgence of interest in certain instruments within our churches in the past few years. Some attribute this as an attempt to appeal to younger generations. While that may be true in part, I view it as a return to the praise methods of long ago, particularly to the time of David. Those people used whatever instruments were available to them at the time. Notice that David ends Psalm 150 (and the entire book of Psalms, for that matter) with "Let everything that has breath praise the Lord" (verse 6). David realized it was the person *playing* the instrument—the one with breath—who was praising God. The instrument was merely a tool.

TO THE POINT

Audible Ways to Worship

- playing an instrument
- clapping

Another audible way to praise is clapping. Interestingly, there are twice as many references to nature clapping its hands in praise than there are to people. Our verse is Psalm 47:1: "Clap your hands, all you nations; shout to God with cries of joy."

Although I normally wouldn't build a belief on just one verse, I am inclined to make an exception in this case. Here's why: David was clearly speaking of clapping our hands. And we should really only need one reference to something as obviously spelled out for us as this. Here's another reason: The two verses about nature clapping its hands are Isaiah 55:12: "The trees of the field will clap their hands," and Psalm 98:8: "Let the rivers clap their hands." If God is pleased with trees and floods clapping for joy, how much more would he love to hear us doing it?

Perhaps when you clap you struggle at times with staying on the beat (or off the beat as the case may be). Don't worry; none of the biblical references to clapping include the necessity of rhythm. I love how one worship leader put it: "Some of us clap on the beat; some of us clap off the beat. The rest of us clap somewhere in the cracks!" Again, the important thing is to clap with joy in your heart to your awesome Creator.

You may have noticed I haven't drawn attention to the fact that certain ways to praise may be controversial. The reason for this is simple: Our focus in this study is not about being the least or the most controversial. I don't want us to even consider that during these weeks. Our goal must be obedience to God, pure and simple. What he says is what we will do.

In addition, I have heard Bible teachers and preachers misconstrue these ways to praise. They make them out to be commands that we *have* to fulfill if we are to please God. But God's only requirement of us is that we *praise* him. We are given eight wonderful ways to do just that and then exhorted to try them. Based on our personalities, some will work better for us than others.

However, I do want to emphasize something here: Just because certain ones seem strange or uncomfortable is not a reason not to at least *try* them. Remember, praise is a "sacrifice" (Hebrews 13:15).

My Daily Praise

Think of an upbeat praise hymn or chorus that you know and enjoy. Sing it out loud before God now. As you do, try clapping your hands with the song. This may feel awkward if, like me, you lack rhythm. But try it anyway. Clap hardily. Clap enthusiastically. Finish your song by clapping as you would applaud a great artist or athlete. God is bigger and more awesome, so your clapping should be even noisier!

My Daily Surrender

Perhaps you're tempted to see some of these various ways to praise as trite, uncomfortable, unnecessary, or even beneath you. If so, please reread the Scriptures pertaining to them. Then consider your body of flesh as dead and your spirit alive to Christ. From that perspective, you should have little problem proceeding with your daily exercises of praise.

Write a prayer of surrender now concerning your personal praise life. Ask God to help you willingly and joyfully try all eight expressions of praise.

JOURNAL

1. Jack R. Taylor, *The Hallelujah Factor* (Nashville, TN: Broadman Press, 1983), 83.
2. W.E. Vine, et al., *Vine's Complete Expository Dictionary of Old and New Testament Words* (Nashville, TN: Thomas Nelson Publishers, 1996), 184.
3. Taylor, *The Hallelujah Factor,* 16-17.
4. Ibid., 84.

THE MOTIVATION

Day 1: The One, True God

Of all the weeks of our study, this is perhaps the most challenging for me to write. (How would you like to try to sum up God in five easy lessons?) Of course, we cannot even scratch the surface of who God is. Huge libraries couldn't hold all there is to be written about him. We never will know all there is to know about God. Paul summed it up when he wrote, "O the depth of the riches both of the wisdom and the knowledge of God! How unsearchable are his judgments, and his ways past tracing out!" (Romans 11:33, American Standard Version).

Although a piano has 88 keys, the pitches go much lower and much higher than what is represented by those ivories. Our human ears are limited to a small frequency range, but theoretically the musical scale runs infinitely in both directions. In much the same way, our minds are severely limited as to how much of God we can grasp.

When I was a junior in high school, a youth group invited me to go with them on a mission trip to New Jersey. Each night of that week we held revival services at a local church. My friend and I were eating at a small pizza place one night after a service when we spotted two guys talking in the parking lot. We decided we would invite them to the revival. After we introduced ourselves and explained the revival services, one of them looked directly at me and said, "I'll come on one condition."

"OK," I said, "what is it?"

"Answer this question: Do you worship Jehovah God or almighty God?"

We thought fast and replied, "Well, we actually worship both; they're one and the same."

"Then I'm not coming to your church," he said defiantly. "I only worship almighty God." For the next 30 minutes or so, he proceeded to explain all his reasons for worshipping only almighty God. He spouted opinion after opinion and even quoted a few verses (out of context, I might add). He was so convincing, in fact, that at one point my friend (who was supposed to be helping me) said, "Oh yeah, we believe that, too!" I wanted to elbow him and say, "Hush up! We don't believe *any* of this garbage!" But unfortunately, I had little more than opinions about God myself. That guy actually knew more verses than I did.

That lengthy discourse woke me up to just how little I knew from the Scriptures about my God. I sat up until after midnight that night searching my Bible for every reference describing God I could find. I realized I could no longer take someone else's ideas as my own. I had to know for myself—not so I could win the next debate on this topic, but because God convicted me that he expects me to get to know the true God, the God of the Bible.

D. Martyn Lloyd-Jones wrote that the object of the Bible "is that we may know God and worship Him more truly. And that is really our reason for considering this great doctrine of God, because unless we do understand what the Bible tells us about God, our worship can never be real."[1] Jesus said to the Samaritan woman, "You worship what you do not know" (John 4:22, Revised Standard Version). May that *never* be said of us. I pray that these next five days will whet our appetites to know who God *really* is.

Israel's great call to worship starts with these words, "Hear, O Israel: the Lord our God is one Lord" (Deuteronomy 6:4, KJV). With so many religions vying for our attention and allegiance today, I believe every Christian should sense the responsibility and urgency to learn better how to defend our Christian beliefs. However, our purpose in this study is purely to gain a better understanding of why our God is the Lord over all.

Let's consider again our anchor story in 2 Chronicles 20. Please read verses 5-12. Imagine you knew nothing about Jehoshaphat's God. What phrases or statements does he make that might persuade you that his God is, in fact, the one, *true* God?

Jehoshaphat boldly professed the God of Israel as the only God they needed. He didn't even consider calling on any other gods. Polytheism, or the worship of multiple gods, was popular during that age and continued into New Testament times. The Athenians even had an altar to an "unknown god," just to be sure they didn't miss one (Acts 17:23)! But God said, "You shall have no other gods before me" (Exodus 20:3). When we abandon hope in all other sources and place our faith in the Lord God *alone*, he will always prove himself to be the one and only God. All others are false and useless.

Do you remember the story in 1 Kings 18 in which Elijah challenged the prophets of Baal? He put them to the test, saying whichever god—theirs or his—answered by fire, that was the true God. From morning until night the Baal prophets begged their god to answer them. They even cut themselves and shouted frantically. But no fire ever fell on their altar.

When it was his turn, Elijah had a total of 12 large jars of water poured on the offering. Please read 1 Kings 18:36-39. God certainly came through for Elijah. Elijah trusted God for who he is.

Unlike Jehoshaphat and Elijah, some of us need to be reminded that God is God (and we are not).

I want us to look now at two back-to-back confrontations God had with Job. This will involve more reading than we normally do. However, I really believe we need to absorb enough of this amazing passage to get the message God was giving Job—and wants to give us as well.

🐦 Begin by reading Job 38:1-30. Look for the evidence God presented to Job that proves no one can possibly compare to him. 🐦 Now read Job's response in 40:3-5. Notice how this exchange effectively *silenced* Job. This was necessary in order to prompt Job's *next* response.

🐦 Please read Job 40:6-14, God's second confrontation with Job; then read Job's response in chapter 42:1-6. Why do you believe Job responded as he did in verse 6?

When we get a proper perspective of God's most high position, we, like Job, will be silenced by true reverence and awe. And ultimately, as we consider his greatness, we will realize our desperation for him and repent of our doubt and self-reliance.

My Daily Praise

Pray the prayer of Jehoshaphat right now, in your own words. Like Jehoshaphat, first proclaim to God who he is. Second, recall before God some specific ways he has been faithful to you in the past. Finally, boldly remind God of his promises regarding you and those around you for both now and the future. This is an awesome daily exercise. Please don't rush through it.

My Daily Surrender

There is one thing that Jehoshaphat, Elijah, and Job all had in common, one thing that is absolutely necessary for our worship to be pleasing: *faith*. Hebrews 11:6 says, "Without faith it is impossible to please God, because anyone who comes to him must believe that he exists and that he rewards those who earnestly seek him." Ask God to reveal to you any ways you don't completely trust him and him alone. Write your response in the space below.

JOURNAL }

Day 2: Transcendent God

Too many Christians today have become dangerously nonchalant in their approach to God. The modern trend is to view God more as our buddy than as our transcendent, holy, and majestic God. Nowhere in the Scriptures is God addressed as "dear God." He's called Holy Father, but never "dear" God.

Please read Hebrews 12:28-29. Think about how recognizing God as a "consuming fire" should affect the way we approach him.

The Bible is clear that the first and foremost way we need to "see" the Lord is as Isaiah did, "sitting upon a throne, high and lifted up" (Isaiah 6:1, KJV). When Jehoshaphat knelt before God to ask for help in his people's crisis, his opening words were "O Lord…are you not the God who is in heaven?" (2 Chronicles 20:6). In Jesus' model prayer, he addressed God the Father in the exact same way. He said, "Our Father which art in heaven, hallowed be thy name" (Matthew 6:9, KJV).

It must be human nature to want to reduce God to someone more like us, someone we can better wrap our minds around. Perhaps that's why God reminds us several times in Scripture, "For as the heavens are higher than the earth, so are My ways higher than your ways and My thoughts than your thoughts" (Isaiah 55:9, New American Standard Bible). David wrote, "For [God] looked down from the height of His sanctuary; from heaven the Lord viewed the earth" (Psalm 102:19, NKJV). We must never forget that God is *still* way up there looking way down on us below.

Our worship should honor his holy and high position. Jerry Bridges writes, "It is impossible to be devoted to God if one's heart is not filled with the fear of God. It is this profound sense of veneration and honor, reverence and awe that draws forth from our hearts the worship and adoration that characterizes true devotion to God. The reverent, godly Christian sees God first in his transcendent glory, majesty, and holiness before he sees him in his love, mercy, and grace."[2]

Jehoshaphat began his prayer with the children of Judah by acknowledging three specific characteristics of God. These attributes are among what some call God's "transcendent" perfections because only *God* can possess them. They are a part of his nature that will forever be unattainable by humans.

Transcendent Attributes

The first transcendent attribute Jehoshaphat reminded God—and the people of Judah—of was his *sovereignty*. That's a big word that basically means God is ultimately in charge. Please read 2 Chronicles 20:5-6. Notice how Jehoshaphat expressed his belief in God's sovereignty.

Why was Jehoshaphat so quick to recognize the Lord's position over the nations? The obvious reason is the peace of mind it brought the people of Judah to remember that God was able to overcome the armies coming against them.

As Jehoshaphat's words of hope echoed across the Temple grounds where the Israelites had gathered, surely some remembered the stories recorded in their Book of the Law—stories about how God had thwarted the plans of many kings who had plotted against his people. God had proven his sovereignty again and again.

Some of those standing there were old enough to remember a great battle against the Cushites led by Jehoshaphat's father, Asa, about 40 years earlier. Hearing Jehoshaphat pray must have seemed a little like déjà vu to them. Like his son, Asa had "called to the Lord his God and said, 'Lord, there is no one like you to help the powerless against the mighty…we rely on you.'" The frightened Israelites were probably encouraged when they remembered that battle in which "the Lord struck down the Cushites before Asa and Judah." (See 2 Chronicles 14:11-12.)

🐦 Please read Psalm 33:6-11. How do you feel, knowing that God might thwart your plans? Does this frustrate you or frighten you, or does it bring you comfort?

Try as we may, no human can come up against almighty God and win. Pushing against God's plan is like trying to push waves back into the ocean.

🐦 Now please read Psalm 33:16-17. Three of man's most powerful assets—large armies, great physical strength, and strong horses—are still no match for the Lord. God can do whatever he wants because he has *all* the power he needs, an unlimited supply. Another word for this infinite strength is *omnipotence,* which is the second of God's transcendent attributes that Jehoshaphat refers to in his prayer: "Power and might are in your hand, and no one can withstand you" (2 Chronicles 20:6b). Omnipotence has been described as "the will of God being put into operation."[3] Jeremiah 32:17 says, "O Sovereign Lord! You made the heavens and earth by your strong hand and powerful arm. Nothing is too hard for you!" (NLT).

As powerful as God is, how much power he makes available to us is somehow based on how much we realize we need it. It's as though God was just waiting for the children of Judah to give up all human attempts to solve their problem. I believe my favorite statement from the entire wonderful story in 2 Chronicles 20 is verse 12. I can relate so well to Jehoshaphat's uncertainty and helplessness when he said to God: "We do not know what to do, but our eyes are upon you."

One of my favorite biographies is *Through Gates of Splendor,* by Elisabeth Elliot. It's the true story of five young men, most barely in their 20s, who answered God's call to take the gospel to a tribe deep in the jungles of Ecuador and straight out of the Stone Age. After several preliminary overtures of friendliness, the men set out on a crucial January day in 1956 for a meeting with the Waorani people. The missionaries' young wives sat by their radios, waiting for news. But none of the missionaries' voices were ever heard again over the airwaves. Some days later their bodies were found, mutilated. Elisabeth Elliot, the wife of the now martyred Jim Elliot, wrote these words:

"In the kitchen we [wives] sat quietly as the reports were finished, fingering the watches and wedding rings that had been brought back, trying for the hundredth time to picture the scene. Which of the men watched the others fall? Which of them had time to think of his wife and children?…This much we knew: 'Whosoever shall lose his life for my sake and the Gospel's, the same shall save it.' There was no question as to the present state of our loved ones. They were 'with Christ'…The quiet trust of the mothers helped the children to know that this was not a tragedy. This was what God had planned…To the world at large this was a sad waste of five young lives. But God has His plan and purpose in all things."[4]

"But how," you may well ask, "could she be so stoic, so calm in the face of such horrible circumstances? Things like that will strip away people's head knowledge about God. It hits at the very core of us. Just what was her secret?" Well, apparently she interpreted everything through the sovereign will and power of God. Here's what she wrote in the closing paragraphs of the book:

"It is not the level of our spirituality that we depend on. It is God and nothing less than God, for the work is God's and the call is God's, and everything is summoned by Him and to His purposes, the whole scene, the whole mess, the whole package."[5]

God has another characteristic that is impossible for us to emulate. It's not actually stated in 2 Chronicles 20, but it is most certainly implied. When Jehoshaphat called God the "God of our fathers," he was saying, "God, you're the *same* God our forefathers worshipped." You see, God is *immutable*. He never changes. He is always the same. The people of Judah had every reason to believe God would keep a promise he had made to Abraham over 1,000 years earlier. (See 2 Chronicles 20:7 and Genesis 17:1-8.)

Once again, we glimpse an aspect of God's perfection that we humans will never obtain. We change every day. Knowing us, we would either be too busy, too lazy, or too forgetful to keep a promise made long ago. While there are certain qualities of God we can never possess, we can find comfort and motivation just knowing our God is infinitely more than we'll ever need.

My Daily Praise

The Bible teaches, "The fear of the Lord is the beginning of wisdom: and the knowledge of the holy is understanding" (Proverbs 9:10, KJV). What about God causes you to fear and revere him? Write statements of praise and thanksgiving to God for those particular characteristics of the Lord that stand out to you right now.

My Daily Surrender

I recently saw a book entitled *Your God Is Too Small.* I have not read the book, so I do not know its contents. However, the title continues to intrigue me. Let me ask us both this question: Is the God you've been worshipping too small? Do you acknowledge only those attributes of his that you can comprehend? Is your obedience to him often based on your own understanding and approval of his directives? Could it be that your reverence and awe of him have been reduced to mere ritual and obligation? Write your honest response below.

Day 3: Relational God

One of my favorite poems is "A Man Said to the Universe" by Stephen Crane:

> "A man said to the universe:
>   'Sir, I exist!'
> 'However,' replied the universe,
>   'The fact has not created in me
>   A sense of obligation.'"

That may be true of the universe, but it's not at all true of God. For reasons beyond our comprehension he has chosen to commit himself to us, to respond when we call on him, to care for us even when we don't care for him. Paul put it this way: "But God showed his great love for us by sending Christ to die for us while we were still sinners" (Romans 5:8, NLT).

Yesterday, we dimly saw a transcendent God way up there in the heavens. Today, our vision becomes much clearer. We get to see more up-close and personal a loving God who left his exalted place and came down…all the way *down* to us. Just as his sovereign power brought the people of Judah great confidence, knowing God *could* do it, there are certain "relational" attributes that brought them much comfort and peace of mind knowing their God *would* do it.

🕊 Let's go back to Jehoshaphat's prayer. Please read 2 Chronicles 20:6-12 from beginning to end. To me, a single word stands out in this prayer. It connects God in heaven with people on earth. I think it is the most important word Jehoshaphat could have uttered—other than *God*, of course. It opens the door to hope and salvation. This one word was so vital to Jehoshaphat's plea that to remove it would have been like turning off the light inside a deep, dark cavern.

The word is *our*. What a great little word! Had it not been for the relationship implied by that word, the people of Judah could have had no hope. He was *their* God, and they were *his* people (verse 7).

Now imagine if Jehoshaphat had stopped his praying at verse 6. Granted, his prayer would have still acknowledged God as sovereign and powerful. But the desperation and fear in the hearts of those people would have remained. Why? Because they needed assurance that God would make his power available to them. They needed more than the God; they needed *their* God to come down from his lofty place in heaven and save them.

So how did they know for sure that he *would* rescue them from these armies coming against them? As they stood there with their eyes lifted toward heaven waiting for God to answer, how could they be certain God would respond to their cry for help? After all, that's pretty important, wouldn't you say? When you're facing the very distinct possibility of *death*—swords going through you, heads getting chopped off, stuff like that—it's a very good time to remind yourself of some of the reasons you *know* he's your God and why he will indeed come through!

Relational Attributes

The first reason that assured them he was their God was his *faithfulness* to them. There had never been a time in Israel's history that God didn't eventually come to their rescue. And he kept every promise he made to his people. Jehoshaphat reminded the Lord of that in verse 7. He said, "Did you not drive out the inhabitants of this land…and give it forever to the descendants of Abraham…?"

Remembering that must have been a great comfort to everyone listening to Jehoshaphat's prayer—all the times God had fought their battles for them and delivered them from captivities, bondage, and probable death. The list is endless. It's always a healthy practice to recall how God has come through for us in the past.

Several years ago I sat down to read a chapter or two in the book of Judges. I found, though, that I couldn't stop at just a couple. I simply could not fathom Israel's moral roller-coaster ride through those 300 or so years. Again and again God restored them, only to have them do "evil again in the sight of the Lord." (See Judges 2:11; 3:7; 4:1; 6:1; 10:6.)

Judges 2:18-19 describes one of the saddest passages in all Israel's history. Please read it now, and take a moment to think about God's faithfulness.

The astonishing thing is that our God remains faithful to us even when we are faith*less*. That is because of his *relationship* with us. It's the relationship of a loving Father with his child—completely permanent, thoroughly dependable. Hudson Taylor, that great foreign missionary and founder of the China Inland Mission, often said that Mark 11:22 should be translated, "Hold on to the faithfulness of God." That became the motto of his life and work. "When you have no faith in yourself," he would say, "then hold on to His faithfulness."[6]

Another attribute the people of Judah joyfully acknowledged was his *holiness*. When Jehoshaphat appointed singers, he instructed them to praise God "for the splendor of his holiness" (2 Chronicles 20:21). The word here for *holiness* in Hebrew means "apartness, sacredness, separateness."

Many people think of holiness as some kind of weird separation from reality (and from any possibility of fun!). To them the word conjures up—as my friend Scott Dawson likes to say—"images of people dressed in black, carrying 10-pound Bibles, and jumping out of corners yelling, 'Repent!'" Of course that's absurd. Nonetheless, it is true that we tend to think of holiness simply as being without sin. And it certainly does include that. But to say that *God* is holy is to recognize he is perfectly pure. The idea of sin cannot even come into the picture.

So why was God's holiness one of the top three reasons the children of Judah knew he was their God? In a sentence: Holiness summed up his goal for his people throughout their entire existence. God had told them, "I am the Lord who brought you up out of Egypt to be your God; therefore be holy, because I am holy" (Leviticus 11:45). He also laid down numerous laws that governed their behavior. He constantly demonstrated his determination to make them a set-apart people.

Now, here is where some Christians become shipwrecked in their faith. They don't want to acknowledge that God is holy. Sure, it's great to lean on his faithfulness. But any of us who think we can act any way we want and still receive his blessings and protection is terribly misguided. Remember, many of the same people who heard Moses give those laws of holiness out there in the wilderness never reached the Promised Land. God let an entire generation of rebels die out. "Was God still being faithful even through that judgment?" you may ask. Yes, faithful to making his people *holy*.

The words of Psalm 29:2b are almost identical to Jehoshaphat's instructions to the choir—except for one tiny preposition. David said to "Worship the Lord *in* the splendor of his holiness." Obviously God expects some holiness on our end as well—in the way we approach him in worship. God told Moses to take off his shoes because the ground around the burning bush was holy ground (Exodus 3). At Mount Sinai when the law was given, even the priests "who approach the Lord" had to "consecrate themselves," or the Lord would "break out against them" (Exodus 19:22). Uzzah tried to "help God out" when he reached to catch the falling ark on its way to Jerusalem. But God had said not to touch it. When Uzzah did, he died (2 Samuel 6). God's holiness is a very serious thing, and our worship should reflect this. We should never worship God in an unprescribed manner.

We would all be in quite a predicament if not for the last attribute the people of Judah celebrated that day as they marched toward enemy forces. Any ugly, menacing doubt that still cowered in the corners of their minds as to whether he was their God was totally eradicated when they sang their rapturous song: "Praise the Lord, for His mercy endures for-

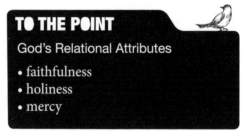

TO THE POINT

God's Relational Attributes

• faithfulness
• holiness
• mercy

ever" (2 Chronicles 20:21b, NKJV). Time and again *our* gracious God has shown *mercy* on his people.

Someone has described mercy as the "holding back" of God's judgment. Now, rather than getting all theological at this point, let me just ask you a simple question: How many times has God held back his judgment on you? How many times did you *not* get what you deserved? If your answer is anything like mine— "too many times to count"—then you already have a great concept of God's mercy.

Read Psalm 103:1-14. "He does not treat us as our sins deserve or repay us according to our iniquities" (verse 10). Although God has not dealt with *us* according to our sins, Someone else was punished for our sins.

Now turn to Isaiah 53, and carefully and slowly read verses 1-6. If you can still see through your probably wet eyes after reading this, here's the question: Who got the job of dealing with your iniquities and with mine?

Emmanuel. God *with* us. *Our* God come *down* to us. No wonder Paul's words practically shout from the page, "Thank God for this gift too wonderful for words!" (2 Corinthians 9:15, NLT). No wonder we call him our *Savior*.

Read 1 John 1:9 very carefully. Do you see how essential a relational, come-down-to-us God is to this verse? In fact, all of 1 John 1 focuses on *our* fellowship with God. That fellowship is only possible because of our *relationship* with him. Take a few minutes to thank God *out loud* right now for the firm relationship you have with him.

David cried out to God, "O Lord, hear my prayer, listen to my cry for *mercy;* in your *faithfulness* and *righteousness* come to my relief" (Psalm 143:1, italics mine). You might need to pray a similar prayer to God right now. If you don't have a relationship with God, admit your need for forgiveness, believe Christ died and rose again for you, and confess him as your Lord and Savior. If you do have a relationship with God but have allowed sins to break your fellowship with him, confess and forsake those now and claim your cleansing as his child. Write your response in the space below.

JOURNAL }

Day 4: Personal God

You know how it is to be driving down the road and have something far in the distance catch your eye. At first you struggle to make out what it is. Then, the closer you get, the better you see it. We've experienced the same kind of thing this week as we've examined our perspective on God. From a distance we could see that he stands out as the one, true God. Then it became obvious that he is much bigger and more powerful than we can even imagine. In yesterday's study we discovered him to be quite approachable. (Actually, he approached *us*!) And our close-up shot of him only made us want to know him more.

Today we'll have that chance. Knowing God in a personal way is actually the highest level of *Emmanuel.* He is not only God with *us.* He can and should be God with *me.* That is his ultimate goal: to be an intimate friend to each of us.

I've been hearing a popular praise chorus recently. The hook line is "I am a friend of God. He calls me friend." I like this song. But we can't just get up on any given day and thoughtlessly mouth those lyrics. They may or may not be true of us at that particular time. Now if the focus were "I am a *child* of God. He calls me child," then that would always be appropriate (if we have accepted Christ, of course). Why the difference? Friendship with God is based on our *present* obedience, while a relationship with him is based on our *permanent* adoption as his children. (See Romans 8:15-17.)

It's sad to say, though, that even worship leaders and musicians, who sing and play for God so often, may not know the Lord as their friend.

Recently I searched no fewer than 20 astronomy books looking for a scientist's view on the wonder of the universe. I couldn't imagine how a person could constantly look into space and not be completely awestruck. Yet all I found were thousands of pages describing specific details of stars, where to find them, theories about how they were formed, and how to categorize them. I couldn't find even one statement about how amazing they are—and definitely no acknowledgement of the God who made them.

Could it be that those astronomers have grown so accustomed to the stars' grandeur that they've missed the forest for the trees (or the galaxy for the stars, in this case)? In the same way, we worship leaders are in danger of merely going through the motions of "professional praise" without connecting on an intimate level with the One to whom the praise is directed. Friendship with a personal God is an absolute *must* for us.

Evidences of God's Friendship

No doubt someone reading this book is thinking, "But how can we know for sure that God *wants* to be that personal? Isn't it enough that he knows my name among those of so many Christians? Now you say he wants to get involved with every detail of my life—where I work, who I hang out with, where I buy my groceries? If I stub my toe, he actually wants to know and help? Come on, isn't that a bit presumptuous, even arrogant?" Well, yes and no: Yes, he does want to be a part of every area of your life. And no, I'm not presuming something that isn't true.

Consider these facts: First, he knows every hair on our heads (Matthew 10:30). (Unfortunately, for me that number is shrinking every day!) Then there are the ravens and the lilies. Jesus said to consider how he cares for them: They don't toil or reap, yet he provides for all their needs. Since the Father does all that, Jesus assured us, "How much more will he clothe you?…How much more valuable you are." (See Luke 12.) The Lord even cares when a sparrow falls. Imagine how much more he takes note of us! (See Matthew 10:29.)

Friendship with God is a *biblical* idea. In fact, it was God who came up with it (of course).

Still not convinced that God wants to be your friend? Then we'll dig deeper…

Read Genesis 3:8-13. Consider how Adam and Eve must have felt during their stroll with God each day before they sinned. Did you notice how natural God's conversation with them was? It's as though they'd spoken many times before in that setting. Evidently, God had already established a friendship with his new creation. Too bad Adam and Eve marred it through their disobedience.

In 2 Chronicles 20:7, Jehoshaphat called Abraham God's friend because God *himself* called Abraham his friend (Isaiah 41:8). I imagine Jehoshaphat was also hoping that God would be the people of Judah's friend that day. They sure needed one!

And what about the *names* of God? The children of Judah recognized their God to be both fearful, powerful *Elohim* and relational, promise-keeping *Jehovah*. This was a good balance for them, and it's also a healthy description for us of what God has in mind for friendship with his people. We are never to view God as our buddy, our pal, just someone we like to hang out with. Whether we're on a stage in front of a thousand people or alone in our homes, God is still *Elohim*, worthy of our fearful reverence. At the same time, we can enjoy his intimate fellowship because he is *Jehovah*. He has chosen to reveal his personality to us. He obviously wants us to get to *know* him.

Our most important and reliable revelation of God was, of course, the advent of his Son. Who better than Jesus to teach us about friendship? He had *many* friends. Certainly he was good friends with his disciples. He spent considerable time with three siblings: Mary, Martha, and Lazarus. Jesus was for all these "a real friend sticks closer than a brother" (Proverbs 18:24, NLT). In Luke 7:34, he is even called a "friend of…sinners."

Three Lessons From Jesus

There are at least three lessons we can learn from Jesus about friendship with holy God. Let's hear from Jesus now as he spoke to his disciples only a few days before his crucifixion. Please read John 15:13. Jesus was about to prove his love for his friends by dying for them. Skip down to verse 16. Who chose whom?

God initiates the friendship. In *Knowing God*, J.I. Packer writes, "*We* do not make friends with *God; God* makes friends with *us*, bringing us to know him by making his love known to us."[7]

The second insight from Jesus' life is that some friendships with God are closer than others. I don't mean to imply that some people get more "cozy" with God or that some might get "off the hook" with God for certain things while others won't. No, we will all stand before the impartial Judge one day and give an account of our lives. (See 1 Peter 1:17.) But there is ample evidence that Jesus was indeed closer to some people than others.

    Please read John 15:15, and notice that, as Jesus' friends, the disciples were privy to special information. He was especially close to three disciples: He chose Peter, James, and John to see him transfigured (Matthew 17:1-2), and he handpicked these same three disciples to accompany him deeper into the Garden of Gethsemane to pray (Mark 14:32-33). Were these three men more "special" for some reason? Not really. But apparently Jesus did trust them more. It could be that he saw in them more passion and loyalty.

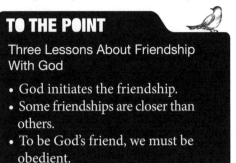

TO THE POINT

Three Lessons About Friendship With God

• God initiates the friendship.
• Some friendships are closer than others.
• To be God's friend, we must be obedient.

One final lesson for us from Jesus' friendships is this: To be his friend, we must be obedient. Jesus couldn't have been more clear: "You are my friends if you do what I command" (John 15:14).

My Daily Praise

Pray out loud now, praising God that he is Elohim, the fearful and powerful One. Then thank him that he is also Jehovah, who wants to be your closest friend.

My Daily Surrender

Ask God what you need to do to be more obedient to him. Willingly submit to whatever he tells you to do. Write that prayer below.

JOURNAL

Day 5: Byproducts of Knowing God

As we get to know God through our fellowship with and worship of him, we begin to realize several benefits. Granted, we should worship the Lord simply because he demands, desires, and deserves it. However, there are some fantastic "perks" to loving and knowing our heavenly Father. In *The God You Can Know* (Moody Publishers, 2001), Dan DeHaan lists several of these benefits. Just try to wrap your mind and heart around this list:

- Character development—Colossians 3:2 counsels us, "Set your minds on things above, not on earthly things." We always become what we worship. If we focus on the world or other individuals, we'll become like them. If we focus on God, we'll become like him.

  Please read Paul's words in 2 Corinthians 3:18. Here's a great summary of this verse: "Gaze on him and be transformed." (If you're not already working on a memory passage, I strongly recommend this one!) As Dan DeHaan puts it, "Find me a worshiper of God, and I will show you a stable man with his mind in control, ready to meet the present hour with refreshment from above."[8] Now that's the kind of person I want to be, don't you?

- Freedom from intimidation— Please read Colossians 2:6-10. Why do you think verse 7 is so important to keeping us from falling into the trap described in verse 8? We should abound in our established faith. We should be rooted and built up in Christ. And because we are *complete* in Christ, his is the only standard we must compare ourselves to. After all, "If God is for us, who can be against us?" (Romans 8:31).

- Compassion—Rather than trying to "work up" a burden for non-Christians, we quite naturally develop compassion for them as we get to know God and gain his heart. After all, who has a greater desire to see this world come to a saving faith in Jesus than his Father? He sent his Son to live with us. Then God, the Father, watched as his only Son was rejected and crucified. All that grief and suffering his Son endured was necessary to buy us back and give us life. "You are familiar with the generosity of our Master, Jesus Christ. Rich as he was, he gave it all away for us—in one stroke he became poor and we became rich" (2 Corinthians 8:9, *The Message*). Yes, I'd say God is invested in those who don't yet know him.

- True satisfaction in God— Please take time now to read Philippians 4:10-13.

True satisfaction is apparently a rare commodity today, even among ministers. Why do we tend to always want bigger and better budgets, choirs, solos, and so on? If our motive is purely to build God's kingdom, then striving for more can be a good thing. However, too often we begin to depend on our successes or other people's opinions to fulfill us. More and more we base our contentment on something other than God. It's no wonder that some people become disillusioned with ministry and fall into affairs or become obsessed with climbing the corporate ladder or drift away from the church.

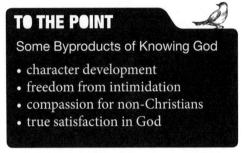

TO THE POINT

Some Byproducts of Knowing God

- character development
- freedom from intimidation
- compassion for non-Christians
- true satisfaction in God

All of these things can be avoided if we come to the right table to be filled. Jesus said, "You're blessed when you've worked up a good appetite for God. He's food and drink in the best meal you'll ever eat" (Matthew 5:6, *The Message*). I've heard that we should never go grocery shopping when we're hungry because we'll be tempted to make unhealthy choices. In the same way, once we've feasted on the bread of God, nothing else is nearly as tempting. (See John 6:33.)

My Daily Praise

Consider one or two of the benefits we studied today. Write a prayer of thanksgiving to God for giving you such blessings and for the opportunity to know him more.

JOURNAL

Paul said, "I want to know Christ and the power of his resurrection and the fellowship of sharing in his sufferings" (Philippians 3:10). Commit yourself right now to knowing God at all costs.

JOURNAL }

1. D. Martyn Lloyd-Jones, *Great Doctrines of the Bible* (Wheaton, IL: Crossway Books, 2003), 57.
2. Jerry Bridges, *The Practice of Godliness* (Colorado Springs, CO: NavPress, 1983), 26-27. Used by permission.
3. Lloyd-Jones, *Great Doctrines of the Bible*, 66.
4. Elisabeth Elliot, *Through Gates of Splendor* (Wheaton, IL: Tyndale House Publishers, 1981), 252-253.
5. Ibid., 271.
6. Lloyd-Jones, *Great Doctrines of the Bible*, 77-78.
7. J.I. Packer, *Knowing God* (Downers Grove, IL: InterVarsity Press, 1973), 4.
8. Dan DeHaan, *The God You Can Know* (Chicago: Moody Press, 1982), 17.

THE METHODS

Day 1: Our Most Necessary Ability

Have you ever wondered how it would feel to be another person? I wondered that recently while reading a biography of Brother Lawrence. He wasn't rich, famous, or glamorous. He was just a simple cook. But he had something incredibly rare. This is how he described his day-to-day life:

> "This is what being in His holy presence is like. My day-to-day life consists of giving God my simple, loving attention. If I'm distracted, he calls me back in tones that are supernaturally beautiful…My prayers consist of a simple continuation of this same exercise. Sometimes I imagine that I'm a piece of stone, waiting for the sculptor. When I give myself to God this way, He begins sculpting my soul into the perfect image of His beloved Son. At other times, I feel my whole mind and heart being raised up into God's presence, as if, without effort, they had always belonged there."[1]

Brother Lawrence understood the practice of the presence of God. His biographer said this of him: "His soul was resting in God, having lost its awareness of everything but love of Him…Because of this, his life was full of continual joy."[2]

This week we have one goal: to better learn the practice of abiding in God's presence. We will focus less on the how's and why's and more on the do's. There is no better way to learn than to practice. Of course, we won't master the skill of listening to God in just five lessons. Some things just take time. However, for us to have a life "full of continual joy," it's definitely worth all the effort and patience!

The question I want to help you answer today is "Do I have what it takes to hear from God?" But you may first wonder, "Is he still speaking today?" Yes, he most certainly is. He loves us just as much as he loved the saints described in the Bible, and he wants us to know him as they did.

Ways God Speaks Today

There are four primary ways God speaks to his people today. First and foremost, he speaks through his Word, the Bible. Paul urged Timothy to listen to God by studying his Word when he wrote, "All Scripture is inspired by God and is useful to teach us what is true and to make us realize what is wrong in our lives" (2 Timothy 3:16a, NLT). Of all ways God might choose to communicate, the Bible is the final authority.

A second way God speaks to us today is through other Christians. Proverbs 11:14 tells us, "There is safety in having many advisers" (NLT). The Lord often uses God-focused men and women to encourage us and counsel us, and sometimes even chasten us. (See 2 Samuel 12:12.)

A third way God communicates with us is through circumstances. As someone wisely said, "Circumstances drive us to our knees so the only way we can look is up!" The three armies headed for Jerusalem were enough to drive the children of Judah to their knees. The

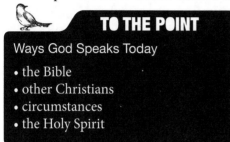

TO THE POINT

Ways God Speaks Today
- the Bible
- other Christians
- circumstances
- the Holy Spirit

circumstances don't have to be bad—sometimes he brings great blessings to get our attention. Paul did say, "The goodness of God leads you to repentance" (Romans 2:4b, NKJV).

One other channel through which our Lord speaks today is his Holy Spirit. Paul certainly knew this: "This is what we speak, not in words taught us by human wisdom but in words taught by the Spirit, expressing spiritual truths in spiritual words" (1 Corinthians 2:13). "OK," you might say, "I know God spoke though his Spirit back then, while the Bible was being written. But what about now? Is the Spirit still speaking to us *now*?"

See for yourself—read John 14:16 and 16:13. Although the Spirit doesn't actually speak out loud, it's pretty obvious Jesus wanted us to know that the Holy Spirit will most assuredly keep on speaking as long as we're in this world.

All right, now that we know that God does still speak today, let's tackle the big question: Can *I* hear God speak? Thankfully, the answer is a resounding yes! No matter where you are in life—even if you don't have a relationship with Christ—you can hear him as he draws you to him. As he did with Saul on the road to Damascus (see Acts 9), God can break through even the hardest hearts and reveal himself to individuals. However, for God to lead us and guide us with his still small voice, there are certain conditions we must meet.

Conditions to Hear the Shepherd

Please turn to John 10. Let's examine that passage to discover how to be *sure* we can hear from the Shepherd.

First, we must accept Christ. We must be *saved*. We have to be *in* his sheep fold. Please read John 10:11. When we place our faith in the one who laid down his life for us, he becomes our Shepherd and we become his sheep.

Now read verse 3. In order for sheep to *listen*, they must have ears, right? The glorious fact is that *all* sheep have ears. The day you and I trusted Jesus as our Savior and became his sheep, we grew some spiritual ears that could clearly recognize his voice.

You might be thinking, "Yes, but I just don't feel *worthy* enough for God to speak to me so directly." Remember, worthiness has nothing to do with it. None of us are "worthy" of anything but death; yet, by his grace, God has given you a good and perfect gift: You have ears.

To consistently hear from God, however, it's not enough just to have ears; those ears must be *sensitive* to his voice.

Now notice verse 4 of John 10. The last part of that verse says, "His sheep follow him…" But how do the sheep *know* to follow him? The sheep "know his voice" because they've heard it before. They've *learned* to recognize it.

We all know that the Pharisees were "dull of hearing." (See Matthew 13:15, KJV.) But did you know that the disciples also had a "hearing problem"? In Mark 8:14-21, the disciples' eyes failed to see and their ears failed to *hear* that they had all the bread they needed. They had missed the point their Lord was making because they were insensitive to spiritual matters. As ministers and leaders in his kingdom we cannot afford to miss such things. We must learn to look below the surface of what we can see and hear with our physical senses. We must discern what God is up to. That kind of spiritual sensitivity takes time to develop.

Just a day or so after they failed their first hearing exam, Jesus gave his disciples another opportunity. This time they passed. When Jesus asked, "Who do you say I am?" Peter answered, "You are the Christ, the Son of the living God." Jesus blessed Peter and said man had not revealed that to him. Only the Father in heaven could have shown him such a deep spiritual truth. (See Matthew 16:15-17.) Likewise, only the Spirit of God can open up God's Word to us and help us understand what the Lord wants to say to and through us. Therefore, we must constantly stay *sensitive* to the Spirit's instructing.

Even with ears open to listen, it's possible we could still miss God's voice. There is one final condition that we must meet in order to be certain we can hear from God: We must *surrender*. The idea here is that we have not only open, sensitive ears, but *bended* ears wanting to receive whatever words of instruction God has for us. Our attitude must be "Lord, counsel me, correct me, teach me, direct me, rebuke me, just please *talk* to me!"

Look at John 10 one more time. Verse 3b says, "He calls his own sheep by name and leads them out." Today's topic is "Our Most Necessary Ability." Being able to hear from God is at the top of our priorities as worshippers and praise leaders for this simple reason: If we don't hear from God, we don't know what to do. He is our *leader*, our Shepherd. We are dumb sheep that need him to lead us.

(In fact, we'd best not take one step unless he *is* leading us!) This means laying down our pride and self-will and allowing him to direct us.

Jehoshaphat and the children of Judah met all three conditions that assured them they could hear from their God. They were saved, in that they were his people. Thus, they had "ears to hear," and they opened those ears to listen. They also showed they were sensitive to his voice when they said, "We do not know what to do, but our eyes are upon you" (2 Chronicles 20:12). Finally, they were obviously surrendered because they ignored all human logic. (What's logical about sending out the choir in front of the army?) They didn't question God's wisdom.

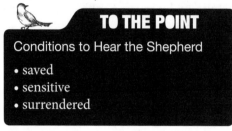

TO THE POINT

Conditions to Hear the Shepherd

• saved
• sensitive
• surrendered

They willingly did exactly what God told them to do. Considering the victorious outcome, I'd say surrendering to his voice was a wise choice for them. It always pays to obey. Just ask Judah!

My Daily Praise

Describe the last sunset you took time to notice. Write down every detail: the shape of the clouds, the colors in the sky, the skyline. Even if it's been awhile since you looked at a sunset, complete this exercise from memory. Decide to stop and notice tonight's sunset and praise God for designing it.

JOURNAL }

My Daily Surrender

A friend once said to me, "I've been asking God for direction, but he hasn't given me any. I hope he's not going to lead me to be a preacher because that's one thing I'm not willing to do! Why won't he just tell me what I'm supposed to do?" With that attitude I seriously doubt he ever got an answer. If we aren't willing to listen to God's voice, why should he bother talking to us? He'll draw us to him and convict us of our sins, but he won't guide us unless we are willing to obey. Like Samuel, we need to say, "Speak, for your servant is listening" (1 Samuel 3:10b). Write down what he's speaking to you, his servant, right now.

Day 2: Our Most Important Asset

What is most important for us as worshippers and worship leaders is that we learn to listen for and discern God's voice when he speaks to us. But for us to really grasp why this asset is so significant, first a climate of *crisis* needs to be created in our hearts.

Now normally, creating such a compelling need inside the reader would be the job of the skilled author. But there are two problems with that: Number one, I'm not that skilled, and two, it's not actually my job anyway. So instead, we need to stop right now and pray and ask the Author of our faith to work in us "to will and to act according to his good purpose" (Philippians 2:13). I'll pray first, and then you can end the prayer.

"Holy Father, we are truly desperate for you to illuminate our hearts right now. We admit we're a little slow when it to comes to grasping what you have to teach us. So make us more teachable. And by your grace we ask you, Holy Spirit, to form our minds and hearts into fertile ground today so the seeds you're about to plant in us will spring up and make us more like you and more effective in your kingdom. Thank you, Lord, for hearing our prayer. And thank you for helping me present these awesome truths. You are faithful, God! I pray these things in your powerful name…"

Now it's your turn. Thank God ahead of time for what he's about to show us…

So what do I mean by a "climate of crisis"? I can tell you very quickly what it *doesn't* mean. It doesn't imply running around, biting off your fingernails, constantly burdened by worry and stress. There are tons of Scriptures that refute that mindset. But a crisis itself can be good; or rather, it can *lead* to good, as was the case with the children of Judah. Instead of pushing them toward a nervous breakdown, their imminent disaster drove them to seek God's help. Their predicament actually catapulted them *toward* that pivotal moment when God broke through the silence and told them what they needed to hear.

Jehoshaphat and the people of Judah had a crisis mind-set—one that says, "We've got a problem—only God can solve it." People with this mind-set have three distinguishing characteristics.

Characteristics of a Crisis Mind-Set

First, they are *desperate* to hear from God. Those of us who are ministers can relate to Jehoshaphat's sense of helplessness. For one, he knew his people were powerless against the vast army bearing down on them. In the same way, our own feeble strength is no match for our enemy, the devil. He hates it when we worship. To deny or ignore his attempts to interfere in our services is both foolish and dangerous. We must have the help of our God, who is greater in us than he who is in the world (1 John 4:4, NKJV).

Read 2 Chronicles 20:3. When Jehoshaphat first heard the news about the coming invasion, he was alarmed. That's the exact moment he switched to a crisis mind-set.

Another reason we know Jehoshaphat felt desperate was because of what he *didn't* do. Read verse 3 again. Isn't it interesting that he actually made a decision *not* to make a decision? He recognized he wasn't smart enough to make the right decision in this situation and had to have God's help. We who are worship and ministry leaders could learn a great lesson from this. It's easy to rely on our experience, our education, and our natural charm to carry us week after week. After a while, we start thinking we don't really need to pray that much. We know that if we were to face a crisis like Jehoshaphat's, *then* we would pray hard. But that's exactly the point: We *do* face a crisis like his. We're leading men and women into spiritual battle every week! Our own smarts are grossly inadequate; we must rely on the Lord's constant direction.

I believe Jehoshaphat felt most desperate when he thought of the people he was responsible for. No doubt, they were shaking with fear. What could he possibly do that would give them hope and help? He could—and did—lead them to seek God.

The children of Judah faced a serious and obvious problem. Sometimes, though, the calamities looming all around us are not so obvious. That's because our crises are of a spiritual nature. Every Sunday when we stand to sing or play that first song, we're looking into the faces of people in *crisis*. Every day when we go to work or school, we encounter searching souls disguised as happy and successful individuals. But far too many are shaking with fear on the inside.

Some of them are in a crisis of commitment, torn between God on Sunday and the world on Monday. Some are in a crisis of the heart, not caring for anyone, even themselves. Others are in a crisis of significance, feeling worthless and without purpose. Some face a genuine crisis of circumstances and are barely hanging on, hoping for a light at the end of the tunnel. Then, of course, many are stranded in a crisis of faith, teetering between belief and unbelief.

All are drowning people in need of a lifeline. And that's what makes their crisis ours. Surely we won't just stand aside and watch them disappear under the water. If we could sense their cries for help, we would kick into a crisis mode immediately. Why? Because we are Jesus' ambassadors. As ministers, we must help people bear their burdens and find relief.

To bring this idea home, stop now and mentally scan the sea of faces in your congregation. Who out there do you believe is in crisis? Even if you know only their first names or where they sit, identify them in the space below. Then commit to pray specifically for each of them this week. Ask God to give you a portion of their burdens, to allow you to share in their crises.

JOURNAL

As important as it is for us to recognize that we are desperate, desperation alone is never enough. We must also be *determined* to hear from our God about our situations. One might say that desperation gets us off the couch, wakes us from our apathy, and jars us into reality. But it's determination that gets us out the door and heading down the road to find a solution to the problem. Desperation without God-motivated determination just leaves us feeling hopeless.

The children of Judah displayed a crisis mind-set when they didn't settle for being on the desperate side of this difficulty. They didn't just *want* to hear from God, they *had* to hear from him. Jehoshaphat, when he got the horrific news, "resolved to inquire of the Lord." His priority from the very beginning of the crisis was to hear from God. Therefore, he led the people of Judah to take three important steps to prepare themselves to listen.

First, they consecrated themselves to God when Jehoshaphat "proclaimed a fast for all Judah" (2 Chronicles 20:3b). Second, they confessed their need for God. Read 2 Chronicles 20:4. Imagine this scene: people "from every town in Judah," possibly hundreds of thousands, gathered in that one place on the Temple grounds in Jerusalem.

That reminds me of a little habit I've tried to maintain over the years. In the minutes just before I step onto the stage to teach or lead praise, I find an empty room or a corner where I can be alone. There I physically kneel before God. I say a simple "breath prayer" confessing how much I need him for whatever I am about to do. It has been one of the most powerfully refreshing practices I have ever experienced.

Finally, the people of Judah prepared to listen to God simply by concentrating on him; their eyes were fixed on him (verse 12). If anybody could use the excuse that they were too distracted to focus, the children of Judah certainly could have. Think about it: A vast army was intent on annihilating them. Yet they knew this was all the more reason for them to be *determined* to hear from their Deliverer.

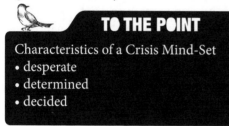

TO THE POINT

Characteristics of a Crisis Mind-Set
- desperate
- determined
- decided

The final characteristic of people who have a crisis mind-set toward God is that they've already *decided* their God is going to speak to them and tell them what he wants them to do. It's not presumption; it's faith. It's not a matter of *if*; it's only a matter of *when*.

When Jehoshaphat had finished praying, the people of Judah simply stood there before the Lord. They had *decided* they were going to get an answer from God about their crisis. And they *stood* there until they did.

Before we close the teaching portion of today's lesson, don't miss this awesome truth: The crisis only lasted until the people heard from God. At that moment when God spoke through his prophet Jahaziel, their mind-set went from crisis to confidence. They knew then that the battle wasn't theirs, but God's. After they heard from their omnipotent God, they had the *confidence* to simply be obedient and trust what he had already told them. They could now joyfully say, "Mission accomplished. Crisis solved!"

My Daily Praise

What has God already told you about the resolution of a particular situation you or someone you love is in? Praise God right now for the part that hasn't yet been fulfilled. Write a prayer stating your trust in his word to you.

JOURNAL

Take a few minutes to pray for each person whose name you wrote on page 61. Write a response to what God taught you today.

Day 3: Recognizing God's Voice

At this point, I hope we have settled in our minds and hearts that God can and must be heard by his sheep. But exactly what does his voice sound like? How can we know when God is speaking to us?

Back in my student ministry days, a teenager named Phillip had been involved in our youth group for about a year. One day as we were riding down the road together, Phillip turned to me and said, "You're always saying that God spoke to you; God said this or God said that to you. But I don't understand. I can't tell when God's talking to me. How can you be so sure?" Phillip's searching question was a wake-up call for me. I'd been working with him, trying to disciple him for months, yet I'd never taken time to explain one of the most fundamental parts of the Christian life (and the most precious to me): learning to recognize God's voice!

The Characteristics of His Voice

One of my fondest memories is of my mom's distinct voice calling me to come inside for dinner. Even if I was several houses away, that high-pitched yell got my attention: "Dwaaayne! Come to supper!" (For those of you who aren't well-versed in "Southern-fried" English, "supper" is another word for dinner, except greasier!)

How did I know that it was my mom's voice? I'm asking this somewhat obvious question so we can enumerate some less-than-obvious answers. There were actually four characteristics that assured me that voice in the distance was indeed my mom's.

First of all, my mom's voice was *familiar* to me. I'd heard it many times before and could distinguish it from everyone else's. The Shepherd's voice is also a familiar voice.

Let's return now to John 10. Read verses 4 and 5. The sheep follow the shepherd's voice because they've heard his voice before, and they've learned to recognize it. Even a newborn baby will sometimes turn toward its mother when she speaks because the baby has heard her familiar voice so many times before birth.

Second, my mom's voice was not only familiar, it was also *personal*. She clearly said my name: Dwayne. Likewise, when God speaks to us, he wants us to know exactly who he's talking to. So he calls us by name.

Read the last part of John 10:3. Jesus says the shepherd calls his sheep *by name*.

Third, my mother's voice was easy to recognize because it was *simple* and *clear*. What if she had said, "Dwayne, I implore thee to make haste and move in the general direction of thy homestead with the express purpose of finding sustenance and renewed energy for thy body"? I would have said, "Do what?" I'm thankful that our God knows our level of understanding, aren't you? He willingly puts his words in a language even *I* can comprehend!

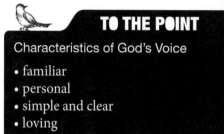

TO THE POINT

Characteristics of God's Voice

- familiar
- personal
- simple and clear
- loving

Now read John 10:9. How much more *simple* can words be? Anyone can comprehend them.

There is one other characteristic I could always count on in my mother's voice: It was *loving*. I knew that behind her words was a pure love and commitment to nurture me. Even when her voice was raised in correction or frustration, her words ultimately served to make me better. (Of course, the belt she used on me did its part, too!)

Notice the love and grace in Jesus' words in John 10:10-11. The thief (Satan) wants only to steal, kill, and destroy us. But Jesus' goal for us is to live fully.

Many of us walk around feeling guilty and condemned for sins we've already confessed to God. Despite our attempts to believe God has forgiven us (as he promises he does), something inside us keeps recalling those sins and shortcomings, pushing us down even further. That "something" is actually some*one*: His name is Satan, the "accuser of our brethren" (Revelation 12:10, NKJV). He seeks to condemn us with his words. The Lord, by contrast, will never speak to us to condemn us. He wants only to give us *abundant* life. Even when he's rebuking us, his purpose is still ultimately to make us more like his Son (Romans 8:29).

(I realize that some reading this right now actually grew up hearing condemning and hateful words from those you respected and cared for the most. You may find it particularly difficult to imagine a God whose every word to us is motivated by pure, selfless love. I encourage you to allow those words in

John 10:10-11 to pour over you at this moment. Go back and read them again. Allow the *good* Shepherd to speak words of encouragement to your soul. Imagine him speaking those words to you *right now*. Actually, you don't have to imagine it. He really *is* speaking to you in his amazing language of love.)

The Contents of His Words

To be sure we are discerning God's voice, however, we need to not only consider the characteristics of God's voice; we also need to examine the content of his words.

Charles Stanley, in his classic book, *How to Listen to God,* cites five criteria for confirming the voice of God in our lives:

1. God's voice is always consistent with the Bible. (God will never tell us to do anything that contradicts his written Word.)

2. God's voice might conflict with human wisdom. (God's ways do not always make sense to us.)

3. God's voice will likely clash with our fleshly nature. (Our old carnal selves will want to do just the opposite.)

4. God's voice may challenge our faith. (God will consistently stretch us to reach higher levels of belief.)

5. God's voice will often require us to be courageous. (Doing God's will is not for wimps. Obeying him will often require bold action.)[3]

Now let's read Jahaziel's words in 2 Chronicles 20:14-17 in light of these criteria.

It's clear that the words the people of Judah received that evening were most certainly God's specific instructions to them in their situation. After hearing from the prophet, they were to go back home and rest in preparation for the battle. Even so, I'm fairly sure some of them still tossed and turned that night. On the eve of possible annihilation, they needed more than a "check-off list" assuring them that what they had heard was indeed God's direction to them. Intellectual confirmation wasn't enough. Their hearts still lacked a necessity: faith.

Jehoshaphat realized that missing element when he said to them the next morning, "Have faith in the Lord your God and you will be upheld; have faith in his prophets and you will be successful" (2 Chronicles 20:20). No matter how much we reason in our heads about God's voice, we still have to make the decision in our hearts to *trust* him.

I remember trying to discern God's will as a teenager. It seemed the more I prayed about what he wanted me to do, the more confused I became. I thought,

"What if the voice I hear is really Satan's disguised to make me think it's God's? Or what if it is, in fact, God's voice, but Satan wants me to think it is his voice, so I won't obey it? Or what if God is speaking to me, but somehow I am misunderstanding what he is saying, and Satan is using my confusion against me?" Whew! What a mess I was in!

In fact, I was so torn by these opposing thoughts that one night during a revival service, I knelt and literally beat the pew with my fists as I cried out to God for clarity. The evangelist saw and heard my anguish. So immediately after the service, he came up to me and said, "You know, you don't have to *beg* God for anything." (I must admit, that made me mad at first. After all, what did he know about my dilemma?)

A couple of days later, I "happened" to be reading in Philippians 3. And that's when I saw it for myself; that's the moment I discovered a principle that has had a most profound effect on my fellowship with the Lord over the years.

Please turn to Philippians 3 right now. Read verses 7-14. Notice what Paul is "pressing" toward.

As I sat there soaking up those Scriptures, I found myself saying, "Yes, God, that's what I'm trying to do, too. I so want to win the prize of knowing you and doing your will in my life!" I had read up through verse 14 many times in the past but had always stopped there. However, this time my desperation pushed me forward. It was actually the very next verse, verse 15, that set me free from my turmoil. What I read there made my heart almost leap from my chest.

Reread verse 14, and continue through verse 15.

Did you catch it? Did you feel the impact of those wonderful words: "If on some point you think differently, that too God will make clear to you"? What exactly did Paul mean? He meant just what he said: If you and I are "pressing toward the mark" with a maturing heart determined to please God, he will not allow us to make a mistake or misunderstand his leading. Hallelujah! No more beating the floor in frustration and hopelessness. I will hear and know his voice. He will make absolutely sure of it. He loves me so much he won't *let* me go astray. What an awesome God we serve!

My Daily Surrender

Ask yourself this: What evidence in my life shows I am pressing "on toward the goal to win the prize for which God has called me heavenward in Christ Jesus"? Write a prayer to the Lord asking him for greater passion to press on. Then ask him to help you trust him to always tell you when your thinking is wrong or you're heading in a wrong direction.

My Daily Praise

Which of God's awesome attributes are you most grateful for at this moment? Since it's *his* praise we're giving back to him, why not ask God right now to lead you in words of praise to him? Pray as David prayed: "O Lord, open my lips, and my mouth will declare your praise" (Psalm 51:15). Write your praise in the space below.

Day 4: Fine-Tuning Our Ears

I am thankful to God that, as we learned yesterday, he will find a way to speak to me as I determine to live for him. But to what length must he go to get my attention? Will it require adversity or trauma? God has been known to speak through a burning bush or a donkey when necessary. I've heard people say, "I guess I just had to learn the hard way." But did they? Could their stress and turmoil have been avoided had they been listening more closely at the outset? That's why it's not enough for us to have ears that will *eventually* hear God's voice. We must have ears that can most *easily* hear his voice and respond to it.

Turn to 2 Chronicles 20:13-15. Notice how quickly and confidently Jahaziel responded to the Spirit's leading. Such ability to listen didn't come naturally to Jahaziel. It came because he had trained or "fine-tuned" his spiritual ears.

Fine-tuning our spiritual ears is very similar to fine-tuning a piano by ear. Although many piano tuners today use electronic devices, a few still tune the old-fashioned way: with just an Allen wrench, a tuning fork, and some well-honed eardrums. I am amazed that they have so developed their hearing that they can sense even the slightest variations in pitch.

In the same way, we must sensitize our spiritual ears to hear every prompting by the Holy Spirit. There are basically three disciplines that we, like piano tuners, have to develop in order to do this.

Three Disciplines for Fine-Tuning

First, we must *practice listening*. This may seem obvious. But how much effort do we actually put into expectantly listening for and discerning God's voice? How many mornings do we awake ready to listen in case our Lord wants to speak to us? How often do we lie awake at night and remember God and think of him "in the night watches"? (See Psalm 63:6, NKJV.) Think about yesterday. How many times did you stop to deliberately listen for God or ask him to speak to you? Was it once, twice, 10 times, or *not at all*? The old adage applies: Practice makes perfect—or, at least, better. We can't expect to grow in our sensitivity to God's speaking if we're not constantly listening.

Even prophets had to learn to recognize God's voice. Samuel was one of the greatest prophets in the Old Testament. The Lord spoke to him often. In fact, passages like 1 Samuel 16, in which God tells Samuel whom to reject and whom to anoint as the new king of Israel, might lead some to the wrong conclusion. From those accounts, they may assume that Samuel naturally recognized God's voice from the beginning of his ministry. But that's not the case.

Please read about Samuel's calling from the Lord in 1 Samuel 3. What about this passage indicates that Samuel had not yet learned to recognize God's voice?

When God first called Samuel by name, Samuel thought the voice was Eli's. It's important to note that Samuel *heard* a voice but could not yet *discern* whose voice it was. That would take both time and practice to learn. If prophets like Samuel and Jahaziel needed to develop their listening skills, so must we as God's ministers today.

Here are two important instructions to help you as you practice listening:

1. Be consistent. Decide right now to "Pray without ceasing" (1 Thessalonians 5:17, NKJV). Stay attentive to the Lord every day. Like Samuel, learn to say, "Speak, Lord, for your servant is listening" (NAS). Create habits like waking up and making your very first words, "Good morning, Lord! How can I serve you today?" It can take years to develop one's hearing so as to properly tune a piano. That represents many days and many hours of intense listening to notes and pitches as they ring out through the air. Likewise, it will take hours of listening with your heart to learn how to most easily and quickly recognize the voice of our God. So be patient with yourself. God is!

2. Be careful. Do not ignore the scriptural characteristics of his voice and the necessary contents of his words. Before you respond in any

way, run that "checklist" in your mind. Take the time necessary to be sure. God will wait on you. Remember, the powers of darkness will seek to deceive you. That's why as Christians, we must never abandon the fundamental disciplines needed to discern God's voice.

The second fundamental discipline in fine-tuning our spiritual ears is to *focus our thoughts*. To tune a piano by ear requires total concentration on the sounds being produced. Hearing God's voice requires concentration as well. Jehoshaphat and the people of Judah obviously understood that. They focused their minds totally on God. That is what Jehoshaphat meant when he said, "Our eyes are upon you" (2 Chronicles 20:12b).

To help us better appreciate their amazing feat, do this right now: Think only thoughts about God for one full minute. Allow no other thoughts to clutter your mind. Focus on him. Ready, get set, think!

So how did you do? It wasn't all that easy, was it? What percentage of your thoughts were either about God or toward God—50, 70, maybe 90 percent? I daresay none of us could claim a 100 percent God-focus. I admit, the first time I tried that little exercise I failed miserably! I was amazed by how many other thoughts battled for my attention. Such struggles with our thoughts remind me of when Jesus asked the disciples in the Garden of Gethsemane, "Could you not keep watch for one hour?" I can imagine Jesus saying, "Can you not keep watch (over your thoughts) for even one *minute*?" He went on to caution his disciples. That same warning should be sobering to us: "Watch and pray so that you will not fall into temptation." (See Mark 14:37-38.)

Paul said we are to "take captive every thought to make it obedient to Christ" (2 Corinthians 10:5). Notice Paul *didn't* say that every thought had to be Christ-like. That is impossible since Satan will, at times, shoot rogue and evil thoughts into our minds. Rather, the instant a thought enters it must be seized and checked. If it is God-honoring, it stays. If that thought might dishonor the Lord, it must immediately be thrown out. Unless we watchfully discipline our minds in this way, we will find ourselves constantly tormented by conflicting ideas and distracted by devilish notions.

Another word that we could call improper and unbridled thinking is "noise." Can you imagine a piano tuner trying to tune your church piano while a CD is blaring out of your sound system? Unfortunately, too often we allow the "noise" of this world, our flesh, and the devil to crowd out the "still small voice" of God (1 Kings 19:12, NKJV).

There is one final but important discipline that we must practice if we are to most easily hear God's voice when he speaks to us. We must *respond to every impulse from the Holy Spirit*. Second Chronicles 20 is replete with examples of this: When Jehoshaphat heard that the enemy armies were coming, he *responded* by saying, "Let's seek God." When the people of Judah and Jerusalem got the call to fast and pray, they *responded* by coming "from every town in Judah." When Jehoshaphat prayed, every man, woman, and child *responded* by standing and waiting before God. When the Spirit of the Lord came upon Jahaziel, he *responded* by speaking what he was told. When Jehoshaphat and the people of Judah heard God's message to them through his prophet, they *responded* in praise.

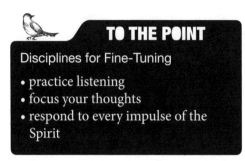

TO THE POINT

Disciplines for Fine-Tuning

- practice listening
- focus your thoughts
- respond to every impulse of the Spirit

Likewise, as we *respond* to every prompting from God, we will sensitize our spiritual ears to his voice. We'll learn to recognize even the gentlest whisper from his Spirit. In a loud and fast-moving worship service, that level of sensitivity and responsiveness is absolutely necessary for every person involved—from the main leader and the instrumentalists upfront to the production crew in the back. (It's important to note what will happen if we *stop* responding to his voice. Rather than becoming more sensitized, our hearing will actually grow *dull*. We could then become a source of confusion and a hindrance to the Holy Spirit's moving in a service.)

Oh God, give us responsive ears that hear you *easily* and *quickly!*

My Daily Praise

Look out a window or go outside and look up at the sky. Purposely comment on how the sky looks. Then respond to what you see by praising God. This will help you become more sensitive to important things that you may have often failed to notice. (How many awesome, God-praising skies have gone unnoticed as we hurry through our lives?)

My Daily Surrender

An old advertisement said, "If you want to get someone's attention, whisper." In reality, however, the only "someone" who will hear a whisper in a loud room is the one looking and listening for it. In the space below, write a prayer, asking God to fine-tune your hearing so that you will hear every prompting of his Holy Spirit today. Then promise to respond with obedience and deliberate praise.

JOURNAL

Day 5: Expecting to Hear

This week we have "spiraled up," as Robertson McQuilkin would say.[4] We have developed a closer relationship with the Holy Spirit. The first day we learned that as Christians or "sheep" we *can* hear from God. The second day we discovered that as worship leaders we *must* hear from our God. On day three, we realized that we *will* hear eventually from the Lord if we meet certain conditions. Yesterday we saw that we can't be content just knowing we will *eventually* hear; we must fine-tune our hearing so we can most *easily* hear from the Lord.

Today we reach the pinnacle of listening, the ultimate goal of our spiritual ears: not just to be able to most *easily* hear, but to most *often* hear from our holy God. When we deliberately and regularly put ourselves in a position to listen, God can download into us his truths, insights, and directives as often as he wants. Richard Foster calls these purposeful listening and learning sessions spiritual disciplines. They include meditation, prayer, fasting, study, simplicity, solitude, submission, service, and corporate worship.[5]

We've invested all week studying *how* and *why* to listen. Now it's time to do what we've talked about. So *listen.* Do you sense God speaking to you?

Talk to God now. But conserve your words. This time is reserved mostly for *listening.* In just a sentence or two, ask him to reveal himself to you today. Tell him something you're thankful for. Praise him briefly. But that's it. Now go back to *listening* closely.

As we go through this lesson, confess any known sins as God brings them to your mind. Speak them, forsake them, then *listen* some more.

Now slowly read these passages: Psalm 46:10; Isaiah 26:4; Psalm 37:7. Meditate on every word. *Listen* for God's still small voice.

Read Luke 10:38-42. Who did Jesus commend: Martha, who was distracted by all the preparations that had to be made as she hosted Jesus in their home, or Mary, who simply sat still at the Lord's feet *listening* to what he said?

Prayer is communicating with God in both directions. He talks; we listen. We talk; he listens. At this moment the priority is on listening to *him* speak. Decide now to only speak when spoken to. Like Jesus, our resolve must be to "say whatever the Father tells [us] to say" (John 12:50, NLT). Our goal, then, is to respond, not initiate. So we listen…

Please open your Bible to Psalm 23. I want to share with you five steps that have been my most effective way of connecting with God during my quiet times over the years. No devotional book, no Bible study, nothing has had a greater impact on my personal growth than this approach: God and me alone with just a Bible and a notepad. Grab your own notepad or journal and get ready.

1. Read the passage completely; then pray a brief prayer asking God to reveal his Word to you right now.

2. Do you see a key theme in this passage? Write it down.

3. Write down two or three key verses or parts of verses that support this theme.

4. Take some time to write down what God said to you through this passage.

5. Then write your response to God.

What we did just now was simply to focus our complete attention on the Lord and his Word. That's what Jehoshaphat and the children of Judah were doing when they purposely placed themselves in a position to hear from God. That's also what Jesus did. He listened often (see Mark 1:35).

There are many accounts in the Gospels in which Jesus rose early to invest time alone with his Father. Perhaps that was when he often received those words he spoke that he said were from his Father. (See John 14:24.)

Phillip Keller, himself a shepherd, sheds some light on this statement in Psalm 23:2: "He leads me beside the still waters" (KJV) Keller wrote:

> "There is no more resplendent picture of still waters than the silver droplets of the dew hanging heavy on leaves and grass at break of day. The good shepherd, the diligent manager, makes sure that his sheep can be out and grazing on this dew drenched vegetation…In the Christian life…those who are often the most serene, most confident and able to cope with life's complexities are those who rise early each day to feed on God's Word."[6]

Our goal is not just to have a "quiet time" that we can check off our list of things to do. Our goal every day is to connect with almighty God. We must wait before him, giving him every opportunity to speak. Andrew Murray says, "I feel that my success during the day will depend upon my time spent alone with Him in the morning. Meditation and prayer and the Word are secondary to this purpose: renewing the link for the day between Christ and me in the morning hour."[7]

Our education in listening has just begun. In fact, in the "art of listening school" we're all just freshmen! I echo Richard Foster who said, "I, too, am a beginner, even and *especially* after a number of years of practicing every Discipline."[8] School's still in session. We must never stop learning how to *listen*.

I remember that day as a 15-year-old when I surrendered to God's leading and began the daily discipline of placing myself before God to hear from him. From that moment, my spiritual growth skyrocketed! How he leads you to discipline yourself may be different from how he led me. Nonetheless, he wants us *all* to regularly carve out time with him.

My Daily Surrender

Enough reading. Stop now. Bend your knees. Bow your mind, your emotions, your heart before the Lord. *Listen* quietly, attentively. Surrender to whatever he may instruct you to do. Write your thoughts before him now.

{ JOURNAL

My Daily Praise

Praise him *out loud* for speaking to you today. What a privilege that he would care enough for us to take time for us! Thank him in advance for how he may prompt you today to help someone else or share your faith with a person who needs to know of his hope.

{ JOURNAL

1. Brother Lawrence, *The Practice of the Presence of God* (New Kensington, PA: Whitaker House, 1982), 38. Used by permission.
2. Ibid., 21.
3. Charles Stanley, *How to Listen to God* (Nashville, TN: Thomas Nelson Publishers, 1985), 51-54.
4. Robertson McQuilkin, *Life in the Spirit* (Nashville, TN: LifeWay Press, 1997), 6.
5. Richard J. Foster, *Celebration of Discipline* (San Francisco: HarperSanFrancisco, 1988).
6. Phillip Keller, *A Shepherd Looks at Psalm 23* (Grand Rapids, MI: Zondervan Publishing House, 1970), 52.
7. Andrew Murray, *The Inner Life* (Springdale, PA: Whitaker House, 1984), 9.
8. Richard J. Foster, *Celebration of Discipline*, 2.

Day 1: Prayer, Prayer, Prayer

Every time I read 2 Chronicles 20, a little part of me wishes I could have been present to experience that amazing worship service. Of course, that's not possible. What is possible, however, is to learn from Jehoshaphat and the people of Judah. What did they do during that service? How did they prepare? What made that worship gathering so successful and powerful? Certainly God did—and still does—the supernatural part, the life-changing part. But what does he expect from us? What is *our* part?

This week we will discover that there are five distinct principles in our anchor story that are also necessary within our worship services each week. For our services to be the most God-honoring and effective, we can't leave out even one of these.

Conveniently, all of these elements start with the letter "p." They are prayer, planned spontaneity, pliableness, power of the Spirit, and pastoral direction. We will start today with the number one priority: prayer.

Prayer

What we desperately need to happen in our worship services is for God to move off the pages of our orders of worship and into the hearts of our congregation. Dwight L. Moody remarked that "every work of God can be traced to some kneeling form."[1] A.T. Pierson, a Bible teacher in the 18th century, once observed that "no revival has ever come about but by united supplicatory praying, as in the Acts; and no revival has ever continued beyond that same kind of praying."[2] It has been written of Charles Finney, a revivalist in the 19th century, that he "unceasingly stressed the primacy of prayer…A man of prayer himself, he would take a strong intercessor with him when he was invited to a city…In a new location Finney would invariably find out who was praying there. He would ask, 'Is anyone here hearing from heaven?'"[3]

The children of Judah positioned themselves to hear "from heaven." Please read 2 Chronicles 20:2-12. Note how important prayer was to the overall outcome of this story.

Jehoshaphat obviously understood that prayer is indispensable. That's why he called all the people to fast and pray rather than to run out and fight. If they hadn't heard from God, they wouldn't have known what to do to win the battle. Furthermore, I believe God honored their determination to seek him first. (According to Matthew 6:33, he still does!)

Not only did prayer have an effect on the outcome of their dilemma, it also had a profound effect on *them*. In fact, at least three results of personal and corporate prayer are revealed in this passage.

First, *prayer puts our focus where it belongs: on God.* When Jehoshaphat prayed, "We do not know what to do, but our eyes are upon you" (2 Chronicles 20:12b), he was placing all their faith and hope in the Lord. I can't begin to count the times I have frantically run around just minutes before a service, trying to get every little detail together. Then I am gently reminded to pray, and my entire perspective changes. I have had dress rehearsals that would otherwise have been disastrous turn calm and productive by simply stopping to pray. It's not a difficult thing. But it does fly in the face of our self-reliant attitudes.

I remember one particularly amazing, life-altering service that our praise team led. I shudder when I consider how my "self-reliance" nearly hindered God's work there. An hour before, I had done no preparation, no planning, and certainly no praying for that service. I was just going to rely on my "natural talent and immense experience." I will be forever grateful that the Holy Spirit prompted my stubborn and pride-filled heart to finally *pray.*

Carol Cymbala, director of the great Brooklyn Tabernacle Choir, said, "[God] can only bless people who are in tune…with him and with one another. That is why we begin every choir practice with a season of prayer…The choir's ability to minister can never be better than their spiritual tone."[4]

According to 2 Chronicles 20:13, even after Jehoshaphat had finished his prayer, every man, woman and child remained standing, waiting to hear from the Lord. Apparently they had been in that position before: desperately needing a word from God. They somehow knew to *listen* for his instructions. Thus, the second result of prayer that we learn from this story is that *prayer sensitizes us to God's voice.*

As we studied last week, if there's one skill more important than any other for a praise leader, it is the ability to listen and *recognize* the voice of the Shepherd. Worshippers should be so familiar and sensitive to his speaking that the slightest prompting is recognized and heeded. I cannot over-emphasize this. I am convinced that the more we learn to listen to God's voice and obey him without hesitation, the more God will entrust to us opportunities to lead his people in praise.

Verse 13 implies that the people of Judah were *silent* before the Lord for a long period of time. This is a powerful idea, especially today, when we seem surrounded by noise from the television, cell phone, stereo—something. It's rare to see a person walking quietly alone in a park or sitting silently by a stream. Some of us actually avoid being quiet.

Yet it's in the solitude of silence that we most often hear from God. In his book *Intimacy with the Almighty*, Charles Swindoll writes, "If we refuse to provide pockets of silence in our lives, we will always flounder in a fog, wondering who God is and what he's doing…But if we deliberately fashion protracted periods of silence, we will grow deeper in an increasing awareness of the real presence of God."[5]

For this reason I want you to take a day to *get away*. Please set aside a day within the next two or three weeks if at all possible. Block out at least four uninterrupted hours to listen to your God. Be sure to take your Bible, this book, and a pen to write down what God shows you. This time alone is of utmost importance!

The third outcome of prayer that Jehoshaphat and the children of Judah apparently knew and certainly discovered is that it *gets results*. God heard, answered, and saved his people as a result of their prayers. We have in our possession the same powerful and effective tool.

Please take a moment to read the following promises about prayer: Jeremiah 33:3; Matthew 7:7-8; John 15:7; 1 John 5:14-15; and James 5:16. Consider memorizing the verse that affects you the most.

Without a doubt Billy Graham will be remembered by many as the most significant Christian of the 20th century. His crusades have reached millions for Christ. Dr. Graham attributes this great success to prayer. One of his favorite and most famous quotes is "The three most important things we can do for a Crusade are to pray, to pray, and to pray."[6]

Sterling Huston, Dr. Graham's longtime Director of Crusades, tells the story of a service during the 1984 Alaska Crusade in which Dr. Graham was struggling with a throat problem. As he started to preach, his voice gave out without warning. Many people immediately began to pray. Dr. Graham called on someone else to preach in his stead that night. When Dr. Graham returned to the podium to give the invitation he could barely speak. Even so, they had one of the largest responses of the entire week that night. As Sterling Huston explains it, "A Team member said to Billy Graham, 'The Lord received glory for Himself tonight.' Mr. Graham's response was 'Yes, He did, and it shows where the real power comes from!' "[7]

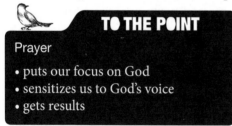

TO THE POINT

Prayer

- puts our focus on God
- sensitizes us to God's voice
- gets results

It's no wonder that prayer is the most necessary element for an effective worship service. That's where "the real power comes from!"

My Daily Praise

Meditate on the verse about prayer you selected. Write a prayer of thanksgiving and praise to God for hearing and answering your prayers.

JOURNAL }

My Daily Surrender

The key to the success of the children of Judah's prayer was their consecration. Prayer for them was indeed a lifestyle. Unlike the shallow and meaningless prayers that godless people cast toward heaven when they see no other way out of a problem, this prayer came from faithful people who had surrendered to God's will.

E.M. Bounds writes, "Consecration is really the setting apart of one's self to a life of prayer. It means not only to pray, but to pray habitually, and to pray more effectually…Consecration brings answer to prayer…God can afford to commit Himself to those who have fully committed themselves to Him in prayer."[8]

So how's your lifestyle been lately? Are you fully committed to prayer? If so, write a prayer asking God to keep you clean and faithful. If not, confess and surrender completely to God.

Day 2: Planned Spontaneity

I want us to begin today with a focused prayer: "Heavenly Father, please open our spiritual eyes to see and our hearts to receive what you want to reveal to us today. We lay down our preconceived notions and opinions. We confess that throughout the years we have formed habits and rituals that aren't confirmed by Scripture. Forgive us for taking someone else's word for what we do as praise leaders. We want your Word as our guide and final authority. We choose to settle for nothing less. Furthermore, we vow to search your Scriptures 'as hidden treasure' until we know for sure that what we believe and practice is, in fact, sanctioned in your Bible. In your Son's name, amen."

The second necessary element for an effective worship service is sometimes misunderstood or misconstrued. Few aspects of church life have brought more confusion and disagreement than the place of planning and the importance of spontaneity within a worship service. Many might say these two ideas are an oxymoron, that they cannot equally coexist.

Just think of the churches you have visited or been a member of. Some of them probably printed a detailed order of worship for the Sunday services. In other churches it might have seemed that little or no thought had been given to the order of worship. I have been in well over 1,000 churches during my traveling ministry and have yet to see any two fellowships approach planning and spontaneity in exactly the same manner. One always seems to take precedence over the other to some extent.

On the one hand, if you're a choir member, instrumentalist, or production team member, you know how important a written and well-communicated schedule can be. A certain comfort comes from knowing what to expect and how to prepare. A schedule also helps avoid some potential problems and hindrances.

On the other hand, recall worship services you've been in. Which ones stand out in your mind? What made them memorable and life-changing? Was it the fact that they stayed on schedule? Probably not. Was it that the music was well-rehearsed and excellently performed? That may have helped, but most likely that's not what set those services apart. What I believe you'll find consistent in every one of them is a worship experience in which God's presence was evident and people responded to his Spirit's leadership in unpredictable and amazing ways. That was the part that no one could plan for; that was the "God-factor" that we must *spontaneously* obey.

Proverbs 16:9 sums up the idea of planned spontaneity perfectly. Solomon wisely said, "In his heart a man plans his course, but the Lord determines his steps." In our anchor story we have a good example of man planning his course and the Lord determining his steps. Below are the elements from that service's "order of worship" described in 2 Chronicles 20:3-19.

TEMPLE PRAYER SERVICE ORDER OF WORSHIP

Announcements—Jehoshaphat and staff (Proclaim a fast; call everyone to pray.)

Call to Worship—Jehoshaphat (Stand in front of crowd; use natural sound system: lungs!)

Prayer—Jehoshaphat (Include these elements in prayer: who God is, what God has done in the past, what God has promised us, what we need of him.)

Wait Before God (Everyone remains standing.)

Instructions From God—Jahaziel

Confirmation—Jehoshaphat (Signifiy by kneeling.)

Responsive Worship—Jehoshaphat (Everyone kneels.)

Praise Time—Kohathite and Korahite Levites

Dismiss—Jehoshaphat

Of course, we have no way of knowing if anything was written down or handed out. However, it is safe to say that some amount of planning went into a gathering as massive and important as this.

It's likely that in advance of their gathering Jehoshaphat had planned to call them to pray (verse 3a). He had already spread the word to fast, and everyone had been told where to gather (verses 3b and 4). Most likely, Jehoshaphat had planned to start with prayer and had considered the general contents of that prayer. Everything else was completely impromptu. Jehoshaphat prayed, they all waited, the Spirit of the Lord moved a prophet to speak, and then they all responded with worship and loud, joyful praise.

Now turn to 1 Corinthians 14. The Corinthians were apparently rather "free" in their worship. However, some people in their church were edifying only themselves. Paul, therefore, gave a gentle rebuke and some much-needed direction to their worship services. Read verses 26-35. Notice the specific instructions Paul gives that make it clear he is advocating order during a church service. Now look closely at verse 30. Apparently Paul expected that at times there would be unplanned and spontaneous revelations during a worship service.

Paul was teaching that unexpected interruptions—when they are motivated by the Holy Spirit, of course—can be a good thing. He wrote in verse 26 that everyone in the body of Christ has something to offer during worship services. Christians are supposed to be more than spectators! The entire congregation of saints should be willing to participate in orderly, appropriate, and church-strengthening ways.

Paul went as far as to write, "Be eager to prophesy, and do not forbid speaking in tongues" (1 Corinthians 14:39). However you interpret the word *tongues* here, the point remains the same: Paul was obviously anticipating unplanned and unrehearsed participation during worship gatherings. The Holy Spirit should not be quenched either by the one through whom he wants the revelation to come or by the designated leaders of that service. (See 1 Thessalonians 5:19-20.) Nonetheless, all spontaneity must be founded on thoughtful and deliberate structure and planning: "Everything should be done in a fitting and orderly way" (1 Corinthians 14:40). Also, we must "test everything" and "hold on to the good" (1 Thessalonians 5:21).

We must willingly submit to the Holy Spirit's leadership at whatever point he may lead during a service—whether it's on the order of worship or not. Scripture is quite clear that planning and spontaneity can and *should* coexist in each and every worship service we conduct. As someone wisely put it, "We must plan as though it's all up to us, and trust as though it's all up to him." To be most effective as lead worshippers, we must seek a balance between these two goals. Another way to think of planned spontaneity is this: We plan *out* distractions and plan *in* both flow and freedom to *obey* whatever God tells us to do.

It is almost impossible to view certain passages like the one we've just studied without passing them first through our filtering systems of individual experiences, values, and tastes. That is why the Holy Spirit must give each of us illumination to see the truths God wants us to learn. I do not ask you to agree with me (and my mere commentaries). Instead, as a Christian and leader of worship, you must "rightly divide the word of truth" for yourself (2 Timothy 2:15, KJV).

My Daily Praise

How has God revealed himself to you over the past few days? Has he reminded you of his faithfulness through a particular situation? Has he had to be especially patient with you for some reason? Have you witnessed his power or mercy? Take time to speak to him and praise him with your voice for what he has shown you about himself. Don't let your feelings prevent you from doing this vital exercise. Write what you pray.

JOURNAL }

My Daily Surrender

Read John 4:4-10. Jesus stopped at the well to rest, but his plan was interrupted. As with Jesus at the well, what may seem an interruption from our human perspective might actually be an *opportunity* God has prepared for us.

What are you planning to do today? Have you already written out your "to do" list? If so, have you included time for unplanned interruptions?

Thank God right now for the interruptions you will encounter today and tomorrow from other people and circumstances. Ask him to help you recognize his hand in each opportunity. Pray that you will *spontaneously* obey what he has already divinely *planned*.

Day 3: Pliableness

In our last lesson we saw that we should plan as much as possible and then allow for spontaneity during a service. But what happens when spontaneous worship actually occurs? How should we respond when our plans are suddenly changed? The third element that is necessary for a worship service to be effective is the *willingness* to be flexible.

During a major citywide festival in Oklahoma City, I had no choice but to be flexible. It was six hours before the opening night. I had planned the service in detail two months earlier. The festival choir was prepared and expecting to sing a certain number of songs; the praise band had rehearsed; the lyrics in their exact order had been given to our video operators.

Then I got the call. The lieutenant governor of Oklahoma wanted to speak about her relationship with Christ during the festival. The only night she could be there was that very same night. Of course, you don't say no to such a great opportunity—even with just six hours notice. So we reworked two months of planning in a matter of minutes. Here's the best news: The service flowed extremely well, and there was a sense of God's anointing on everything that took place that night. In fact, hundreds placed their faith in Christ as their Savior that evening!

All of us who have planned services probably could tell stories similar to this—times that God got the glory even though our plans got the boot! Of course, it's one thing to be forced into flexibility (as we go kicking and screaming!), but it's quite another to willingly *allow* our plans to be thwarted right before our eyes. That requires *trust*.

As described in 2 Chronicles 20, the people demonstrated their trust in God as they quickly recognized the need to be flexible. Consider this: (1) Jehoshaphat had to be flexible because he'd never fought a battle in this way before—with praise rather than swords. (2) The people of Judah had to be flexible because they'd never stood around waiting to hear, rather than suiting up to fight. (3) The choir had to be flexible because they had never led worship from this vantage point before—from the front lines of an army going to battle.

At first, Jehoshaphat and the children of Judah no doubt felt forced to give up their own plans and turn to God. After all, they were having a normal and comfortably predictable day with everything going pretty much as usual. Then, out of the blue, they got the news they never wanted to hear: Three vast armies were coming to destroy them. (Talk about ruining your day!) They were backed into a corner and had no way to look but up. Most likely, more than a few of the people standing in that huge crowd around the Temple grounds were somewhat bitter about their little "situation."

Frankly, joyful praise was almost surely the *last* item on their priority list at that moment. Yet, with just a few words from one man's mouth, their circumstances downgraded from desperate to merely demanding—demanding of *praise*, that is.

Read the prophet Jahaziel's words in 2 Chronicles 20:15-17. Put yourself in the shoes of those listening to his divinely inspired words.

Romans 10:17 says, "Faith comes by hearing, and hearing by the Word of God" (NKJV). The people of Judah heard the Word of God through his prophet. Can you imagine how relieved they must have been? In the same way, once we've heard from God and know he is directing us through a worship experience, we can relax and trust him to move it any direction he wants.

Let's return to 1 Corinthians 14:30 for a moment. Paul instructed the speaker to stop if he is interrupted. Young's Literal Translation says, "Let the first be silent." Imagine you are helping with a great worship set that your music ministry and technical teams have worked hard to prepare. Before you can finish your complete set of songs, someone in the congregation lifts his hand. When you acknowledge him, he says, "Excuse me, I'm very sorry to interrupt you this way, but I have something I believe I'm supposed to share." Granted, what he is doing might appear inappropriate to some, but according to Scripture, you have an obligation to stop and at least *consider* allowing that person to speak.

Conditions for Spontaneity in Services

There are, of course, certain conditions Paul puts on spontaneous "revelations" in order to "test" them. (See 1 Thessalonians 5:21a.) First, the one wanting to speak must be recognized as in the church. In context, Paul was addressing "brothers" (1 Corinthians 14:26a). By inference, that brother should have a life that evidences his walk with Christ. Second, he should be willing to take his turn and not rudely interrupt while God is speaking through someone else (verse 31). Third, he should be subject to "prophets" or leaders in the church (verses 29-32). (It should be noted that some would also include a fourth test: The speaker should be a man, not a woman. [See verses 34-35.] This can be a divisive topic within churches. It's not possible within this study to adequately examine all the scriptural arguments on both sides of this topic. I encourage you to follow the teaching of your pastor and individual church regarding the role women should play in the service.)

I realize the idea of a revelation suddenly coming to a Christian sitting in the congregation during a worship service seems extremely unlikely. It's certainly the exception rather than the norm in most churches today. I don't believe Paul was necessarily advocating that it become a standard every church should follow. Nonetheless, I believe Paul was trying to burn into our understanding that God can do *anything* he wants through any*one he* chooses.

If God can choose to speak through a layman in the congregation, surely he might speak through someone in a choir, praise team, or orchestra. These people have (I hope) already been proven and tested to be sensitive servants of the Lord. In many of our services, the music minister and pastor do all the talking. We would be wise to encourage other team members and church leaders to have "a hymn, or a word of instruction" to edify the body—even on the spur of the moment as the Holy Spirit prompts them. (See 1 Corinthians 14:26.)

As I've sat down to plan worship services over the years, I've tried to form a few good habits. Perhaps the most important habit is to always start with the statement "Lord, this is your worship service, so please plan it however you want it." I've found this helps me keep my perspective during a service.

Yes, it's true that we as worship leaders and worship teams are responsible before God for what takes place during a service. However, it's still *his* service. *He's* in charge of it. And he is plenty able to protect and lead it. Until we lay aside our preconceived notions of what that service should be and totally yield it to him, we will never be effective worship leaders whom God can work spontaneously through and around.

Trust is the key. We must "trust in the Lord" even when we don't understand him. (See Proverbs 3:5.) During each and every spontaneous moment of our worship services, he will grant us the wisdom, discernment, and direction we need.

My Daily Praise

Today we continue our experiment in demonstrative praise. The Bible tells us to "shout to God with the voice of triumph!" (Psalm 47:1, NKJV). In a moment, I want you to try shouting to God. (You may have to shout in a somewhat subdued way so as not wake up your neighbors or family!) But shout as loudly as you can. Imagine you're watching your favorite team, and it's about to score. Now apply that same level of enthusiasm to your shout of praise to the Lord. He is always "in scoring position"! And we are always on the winning team. You can try a "woo-hoo" or a "yea" or shout out part of a verse or a sentence such as "Thank you, God!" or "You are awesome!" There's no wrong way to do this as long as it comes from a pure and passionate heart.

My Daily Surrender

So how do you feel when your plans are changed at the last minute? Are you sometimes tempted to grumble or be uncooperative if your pastor or worship leader feels led to go in a different direction right in the middle of a worship set? How do you respond when someone wants to spontaneously speak a word of praise for God? To be *pliable* means to be bendable, workable, and moldable. God is waiting for us to let go and let him be the great potter that he is! We must get the service order out of our hands and into his.

Write a prayer asking God to help you trust him and surrender to his work of bending and shaping you into his image. Ask him to increase your spiritual flexibility.

JOURNAL }

Day 4: Power of the Spirit

Without this fourth element—the power of the Spirit—our worship services will have no lasting impact. Only God's Spirit can draw a person to saving faith in Christ (John 6:44), only he can convict the world of guilt (John 16:8), only he can guide us into all truth (John 16:13), and only he can sanctify us to be conformed to the image of God's dear Son (Romans 8:29). Unfortunately, too often the church has downplayed the vital importance of the Spirit in the daily life of the Christian. If we are to be truly effective as ministers, we absolutely must have his Spirit working through us. Zechariah 4:6 makes this clear: "It is not by force nor by strength, but by my Spirit, says the Lord of Heaven's Armies" (NLT).

Jim Cymbala, pastor of The Brooklyn Tabernacle in New York City, writes, "Our attempt at ministry will be an absolute exercise in futility if we are not expecting and experiencing divine help through the power of the Holy Spirit. It is not enough to teach and preach about the Spirit. We must experience him personally in new depths, or we will accomplish little. Without the Holy Spirit there is no quickening of the Scripture. Worship is hollow. Preaching is mechanical, never piercing the heart."[9]

Reliance on the Spirit is evident in the story of Jehoshaphat and the people of Judah. As they waited for instructions before the Lord, "the Spirit of the Lord came upon Jahaziel" (2 Chronicles 20:14a). It was the Holy Spirit who gave the words that caused the children of Judah to rejoice.

Some of the most famous ministers relied on the power of the Holy Spirit. D.L. Moody wrote this: "I was crying all the time that God would fill me with his Spirit. Well, one day, in the city of New York—oh, what a day!—I cannot describe it, I seldom refer to it; it is almost too sacred an experience to name. Paul had an experience of which he never spoke for fourteen years. I can only say that God revealed Himself to me, and I had such an experience of His love that I had to ask Him to stay His hand. I went preaching again. The sermons were not different; I did not present any new truths; and yet hundreds were converted."[10]

While in college I studied the ministry of Jesus as described in the book of Luke. What I found in chapter 4 was nothing short of startling, and it forever solidified my reliance on the Holy Spirit as my source of power.

I want to walk you through this series of verses now just as I discovered them that morning in my dorm room. Before we begin this little scouting mission, please stop and ask God to give you insight and an open heart to what he wants to show you today from his Word.

Read Luke 3:21-22. Notice the Spirit's role in this scene.

Now read Luke 4:1-2. How is Jesus described as he returned from the Jordan? Notice *who* led him into the desert (verse 1b).

Verses 3-13 describe Jesus' temptation by the devil.

Carefully read verse 14. How did Jesus return to Galilee? What happened throughout the whole countryside?

Finally, read verses 16-19. Notice the very first words Jesus read from Isaiah (verse 18a).

Did you notice the Holy Spirit's role in every aspect of this passage? According to Luke 3, Jesus began his ministry the day the Spirit descended on him. Then the Holy Spirit led him and filled him. In Luke 4, the Spirit's power was on Jesus, causing the news of him to spread. And the very first public words of Jesus' ministry credited the Spirit's anointing of him. Furthermore, it was not until *after* the Spirit filled and empowered him that Jesus performed his first miracle. (See John 2:1-11.)

Here is what the Lord whispered to my heart as I sat at my desk that early weekday morning: "Son, if Jesus needed the power of my Spirit to be effective in ministry, how much more must *you* have the Holy Spirit anointing your life?"

We may be tempted to think, "Well, that's Jesus. I could never do the things he did, even with the Holy Spirit." But that's not so. Jesus said to *all* his disciples: "I tell you the truth, anyone who believes in me will do the same works I have done, and even greater works, because I am going to be with the Father" (John 14:12, NLT). He went on to say that he would therefore send the Comforter, the Holy Spirit, in his stead (John 16:7, KJV). Paul prayed that God would strengthen us "with power through his Spirit" in our inner being (Ephesians 3:16). He described the power dwelling in us as the same force that raised Christ from the dead (Ephesians 1:20)!

It's not enough for his Spirit to live in us because we've accepted Christ; we must *be filled* with his Spirit every day. In Ephesians 5:18 we read, "Do not get drunk on wine, which leads to debauchery. Instead, be filled with the Spirit." Every day that is not a Spirit-filled day is a wasted day. In his book *The Secret of Supernatural Living*, Adrian Rogers writes, "In my estimation, the cause of Christ has been hurt far more by Christians who were carnal and not Spirit-filled than by Christians who were drunk."[11] As he explains it, at least people will *know* if you're drunk with alcohol! If we're not filled up with God as we stand to represent him before people, we are doing nothing more than putting our flesh on parade. And here's the scary part: What if those watching don't realize we are full of ourselves? We could literally lead them *away* from God rather than closer to him. Again, we *must* be filled with his Spirit. Nothing less is acceptable as ministers and Christians.

My Daily Surrender

To be filled with the Holy Spirit is really more about getting *un*filled with ourselves. Here are the simple steps necessary to ensure we remain filled with him. (1) We must completely surrender every room and closet of our heart's home. Well has it been said, "If he's not Lord *of* all, he's not Lord *at* all." (2) Then we invite him to come and fill us up with only himself. (3) To continue being filled, we must daily claim his filling and continually surrender afresh to his voice and direction.

Take time to write a prayer surrendering yourself and claiming his Spirit.

JOURNAL }

Tune up your vocal cords and sing a praise song to God right now. Don't just hum it. Let the melody you're making in your heart come out of you like a fountain of flowing water. Remember, he loves to hear you sing! (He should. He made your voice!)

Day 5: Pastoral Direction

You may wonder why I consider the role of the pastor one of the "top five" essentials for effective worship services. Well, we don't have to look very far to see the reason.

What are all the names you remember from our anchor story, 2 Chronicles 20? I am 99 percent sure that the first and possibly only name you remember is Jehoshaphat. In fact, other than a reference once to Jahaziel, Jehoshaphat is the only one who is even recognized in this account. His name appears 11 times in 2 Chronicles 20:1-30. How is it that in a gathering of thousands, one person's actions and words are highlighted more than anyone else's? In a word: *leadership*. Leadership is God's formula for directing his people. Other notable leaders include Moses, David, Solomon, Joshua, Paul, and, of course, Jesus.

Please read 2 Chronicles 20:18-21, paying special attention to how the people's response demonstrates Jehoshaphat's influence among them. It's important to note two things: It was Jehoshaphat who was the first to fall on his knees. He led the way for the others to praise. Furthermore, it was Jehoshaphat who *appointed* the musicians, not the other way around. He even told them what he wanted them to sing. Now, that tends to cause most of us church musicians to cringe just a bit. Who really wants the pastor (or anyone else, for that matter) choosing songs for us?

However, in the Bible, the "overseer" (pastor or bishop) *was* the worship leader—or lead worshipper, to be more exact. Of course, unlike Jehoshaphat, pastors are not kings and should not act like them. Nonetheless, the lead pastor should be involved to some degree in putting together and overseeing the worship gatherings of the church. Even the most talented and experienced music ministers need some level of support, participation, and encouragement from the "under-shepherd" of that flock. This is God's formula for his people. It's a pastor's role to give leadership and direction and to entrust and empower other capable staff and lay leaders to help (and to lead as needed).

Read Acts 20:28. Note that it is the Holy Spirit who gives the pastor or "overseer" authority. Most of us at some point have had issues with authority. And some of us have never quite grown out of our rebellion, especially in the church. I've known of some music directors who actually made it their goal to "get as much time as the preacher each Sunday"! Where is the servant's heart?

John the Baptist's words should also be our cry: "He must become greater and greater, and I must become less and less" (John 3:30, NLT).

Before we can have the blessings of God on our music ministry—or any other ministry, for that matter—we must acknowledge and *submit* to the authorities God has placed above us. (See Hebrews 13:17.) Those of us who are music directors on staff are most likely directly responsible to the senior or executive pastor. If we are a volunteer in the choir, orchestra, or production team, our leader is probably the music or orchestra director. One thing is sure: We are all accountable to certain overseers within the church body.

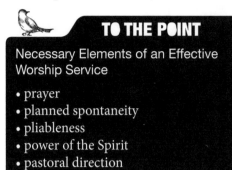

TO THE POINT

Necessary Elements of an Effective Worship Service

• prayer
• planned spontaneity
• pliableness
• power of the Spirit
• pastoral direction

I cringed and was saddened when I read one theologian's conclusion about music within the worship service: "In most instances it is the part of the service least under our control. Many musical directors…have rather independent feelings about the choice…of church music and tend to be somewhat jealous of their prerogatives. But…we [pastors] often hold considerable power of negotiation…and can make suggestions regarding…musical selections."[12]

"Negotiation" and "suggestions" from the pastor, "jealousy" from the music director—how did such concepts find their way into a book on worship? Sadly, far too many church musicians and music directors—I refuse to call them ministers through music—do, in fact, have a rotten and rebellious attitude toward authority.

Please read 1 Peter 5:5. Notice what our attitude *should* be.

My Daily Praise

Our praise today will be for Jehovah-Rohi, which means "The Lord, our Shepherd." This particular covenant name for God appears in Psalm 23:1. Read Psalm 23 now, and after you read each statement, praise God aloud in response. Bask in the knowledge that the "Shepherd and Overseer" of your soul (1 Peter 2:25) leads you, guides you, protects you, and corrects you. Isaiah wrote, "He shall feed his flock like a shepherd: he shall gather the lambs with his arm, and carry them in his bosom, and shall gently lead those that are with young" (Isaiah 40:11, KJV). Praise Jehovah-Rohi out loud right now!

Before we end this week's lessons, take a few minutes to review the five essential elements of an effective worship service. I hope that after these five days of study, you understand the indispensable importance each of these elements plays in a corporate worship service. However, these principles also apply to our everyday lives. In fact, if we want to see these five elements demonstrated in our church services, then you and I must have them in our own lives—for *we* are the church.

Think about what each element means, and then ask yourself if you are personally demonstrating these elements while you're at home and at work or school each day. Write a prayer to God now, asking him to help you strengthen those areas in which you are weakest.

{ JOURNAL

1. Sterling W. Huston, *Crusade Evangelism and the Local Church* (Minneapolis, MN: World Wide Publications, 1986), 49.
2. Ibid.
3. Sherwood Eliot Wirt (ed.), *Evangelism: The Next Ten Years* (Waco, TX: Word Books, 1978), 97.
4. Jim Cymbala, *Fresh Power* (Grand Rapids, MI: Zondervan Publishing House, 2001), 99.
5. Charles R. Swindoll, *Intimacy with the Almighty* (Anaheim, CA: Insight for Living, 1996), 20.
6. Sterling W. Huston, *Crusade Evangelism and the Local Church,* 49.
7. Ibid., 49-50.
8. E.M. Bounds, *The Essentials of Prayer* (Springdale, PA: Whitaker House, 1994), 96.
9. Jim Cymbala, *Fresh Power,* 48-49.
10. W.R. Moody, *The Life of Dwight L. Moody* (Westwood, NJ: Barbour Books, 1985), 135.
11. Adrian Rogers, *The Secret of Supernatural Living* (Nashville, TN: Thomas Nelson Publishers, 1982), 43.
12. Jack Hayford, et al., *Mastering Worship* (Portland, OR: Multnomah, 1990), 119-120.

THE MINISTERS

Day 1: Ministers *Through* Music

The only times many people in our congregations ever see those of us involved in music ministry is when we're on a stage "doing our thing." Frankly, whether we're singing in the choir or praise team, playing an instrument, or waving our arms to direct a hymn, it's not that difficult to make a good impression from that elevation. But being a true minister involves much more than what we do on stage. It's who we are when we walk off the platform. I once heard Charles Stanley say, "We may impress people from a distance, but we'll only impact them as they see our lives up close."

This week we will turn our attention to the men and women behind the titles, beyond the lights and cameras and exciting services. What can we learn from the people God handpicked in 2 Chronicles 20? What qualified them to be ministers? Throughout the next five days we'll examine those and other people in God's Word. They exemplified certain qualities we must all have in order to be the ministers and leaders God has called us to be.

First, please stop and ask God to give you understanding, alertness, and "stick-to-itiveness" as you read and absorb these studies.

I'd like to begin by asking you to carefully consider how you view yourself. During my first semester in college, a music professor posed a question to our class that I had never considered. He said, "How do you see yourself: as a musician who happens to be a Christian, or as a Christian who happens to be a musician?" To me the answer was ridiculously obvious: "Of course, I'm a Christian first!" The professor went on to explain that the way we answer that question will determine how we approach music throughout our lives.

Since then I've come to realize just how right he was. If we view ourselves as musicians first, then we'll tend to sing and play music for its own sake. We may even have an agenda with our music and expect people to learn to appreciate it "for what it is." Unfortunately, this approach could cause us to overlook the very reasons God created music in the first place: to praise *him* and to minister to other *people*.

Four Levels of Effectiveness

I have observed four levels of effectiveness among those who are involved with music in churches. I believe that how we view ourselves and our music has a lot to do with where we eventually land on this ascending scale. As we explore them, ask yourself from which level you most often operate.

The lowest level is what I call the *song leader* level. These are the people who show up and help with a few songs. They put no thought into planning or purpose. They often arrive just in time to throw their music pages together. They prefer to simply play and leave. They avoid rehearsals and planning sessions. They just want to sing or play—nothing more.

I frankly believe God has little use for people who are content to stay at this level, which at best produces mediocrity. These people are "lukewarm" (and you know what Jesus said he would do with those who are lukewarm; see Revelation 3:16). No matter how talented they may be, if they cannot be passionate about their role in worship services, there are plenty of other ministries that could use their involvement. It's better to have 10 people who are sold on music ministry than 100 who are just showing up.

The next level is the *music director*. These are people who want to have input in making the music the best it can be. They are not content with just showing up. They like to be prepared, and they want to know that the music is planned. Their focus on excellence and organization is commendable. They struggle at times, however, with seeing past the music and getting everything just right. They know what and how to sing and play, but sometimes they forget *why* they're doing it.

As Jack Hayford explains, they "become preoccupied with style rather than substance, with how things look and feel rather than with what truths they communicate."[1] Ministry often takes a back seat to excellence and appropriateness. If they were to be honest, their actions and attitudes are probably based on a belief that they are first of all *musicians*.

The third level is the *minister of music*. God can greatly use folks at this effectiveness level because they understand that music praises God and ministers to others. They want their music to change those who are listening, just as David's harp soothed Saul (1 Samuel 16:23). While they appreciate and even strive for excellence (and often achieve it), they are also committed to pleasing and blessing God.

The Levite musicians were mostly Level 3 ministers of music because their priority and their goal were to use their music to minister to God.

Please read 1 Chronicles 6:31-32. Notice what ministry or service they were to perform. Now read 1 Chronicles 16:4. Notice specifically where some of the Levites were to minister. Interestingly, Strong's Concordance defines the Hebrew word translated *ministry* as "service."

As faithful as the Levite musicians were to carry out their duties, their effectiveness as ministers was somewhat hindered. They were actually *limited* in reaching their ministries' fullest potential by two significant factors: First, these particular Levites primarily ministered when they performed their music. Once they had performed their songs of praise, they were finished with ministry until they sang or played again. Second, their service rarely extended beyond the Temple walls. Their assigned place of ministry was before the ark, which was *inside* the tabernacle or Temple. Therefore, they were not particularly obligated to carry their ministry out into the real world. You might say that by nature of their appointment they were "plateaued" at Level 3.

Of course, we as Christians are God's temple now. The Holy Spirit lives in us. Our ministries are no longer confined within a building. We aren't limited as the Levites were. The fact is, to fulfill the high calling God has placed on our lives as his ministers, we cannot settle for Level 3. We must press on to *Level 4*.

The fourth and *highest* level for church musicians (and technical assistants) is to be a minister *through* music. People on Level 4 still desire the excellence of Level 2. Like those on Level 3, they see the great blessing musical praise can be to God and other people. However, Level 4 people realize that our *music* is not the minister; *we* are the ministers. God didn't ordain the music to bless him and others, but he ordained *us* to serve him. And we are responsible to serve whether we're making music or not.

Ministry is more about who we *are* than about something we *do*. Church staff music leaders are often called ministers of music. I much prefer this description: ministers *through* music. That subtle change quickly and clearly reminds me of my role as God's minister. Peter said, "Each one should use whatever gift he has received to serve others" (1 Peter 4:10a). My gift of music or production is merely a tool *through* which I can better serve God and show his love to others.

Level 4 ministers not only view *themselves* as ministers, they also understand that their ministry extends far *beyond* the music they assist with during weekend worship services. They want to be involved in people's lives as God gives them the opportunity. Ministers with the greatest effectiveness in God's kingdom will seek to help people grow in their faith.

If we believe that our *music* does the ministering, once the songs stop, so do our responsibilities to the listeners. We are not obligated to minister to them beyond the "show" from the platform. This approach can foster a personality-driven ministry. Musicians who see themselves as personalities tend to view their ministries as mostly what they do *on*stage. But true ministers are available and want to be used by God even when they're *off*stage.

The singers that Jehoshaphat appointed in 2 Chronicles 20:21 certainly qualified as Level 4 ministers. Many of them were probably Levite musicians, so their "job" was to sing in the Temple. Yet they willingly went way beyond the call of duty as they marched in the opposite direction from the ark and the Temple. They weren't just ministering before the Lord; they were now waging war. Talk about stretching themselves!

A minister *through* music is first and foremost a servant. When I think of people who model servitude through music I immediately think of my friend Kevin Derryberry. Kevin has an amazing stage presence and is one of the most talented vocalists and musicians I have ever heard. He truly has the makings of a superstar. Even so, I caught a glimpse of the "real Kevin" one night during a festival in Knoxville, Tennessee, where I was leading worship. He was a "personality" during the festival and had his picture on posters throughout the city. One night after he'd finished his song set, he came off the platform and began talking to a young mother and her children at the back of the stadium. She wanted to stay to hear Scott Dawson preach but couldn't because she was a single mom with no one to watch her little ones. Right then Kevin the music personality became Kevin the baby sitter. He volunteered to entertain her kids so she could stay for the worship service. She accepted Christ that night, and Kevin led her oldest child to the Lord.

God must smile when we see ourselves as his servants—nothing more, nothing less. Blessing others with a servantlike heart will keep on blessing God long after the music fades.

My Daily Praise

Meditate on Jehovah-Tsidkenu, the Lord, our Righteousness. Read 1 Corinthians 1:30; 2 Corinthians 5:21; and Jeremiah 23:6. Thank and praise God through at least one of the eight ways to praise: singing, shouting, clapping, kneeling, dancing, testifying, playing an instrument, and raising holy hands.

My Daily Surrender

It's time for a "gut check" (to put it rather crudely). How much do you like ministering to others as you stand in front of them? How about when you've completed your music or production duties? How willing are you to serve others *after* the spotlight's turned off? Pray now and ask God to help you evaluate yourself accurately and honestly. Write your prayer response in the space below.

JOURNAL

Day 2: Recognition Is Not Required

The next two days' studies are both based on a single verse: 1 Peter 5:6. Because this verse is so important to grasping what I believe the Lord has for us, I want you to read it now, carefully and slowly.

The first half of this verse deals with humbling ourselves before God. Tomorrow, we will examine the second half, how in God's good time he will lift us up.

I am particularly passionate about these two lessons. As we say in Alabama— I'm "downright" excited about 'em! Sadly, there is very little teaching on these topics. Nevertheless, I deeply believe that fully grasping the truths we will examine today and tomorrow will radically change our perspective of a kingdom musician.

Please turn back to 2 Chronicles 20. (Those pages in your Bible are probably becoming a bit worn by now!) Let's focus on verses 20-23. Notice the role the singers and musicians played during the battle. How important do you think their responsibilities and actions were to the outcome?

Did you also notice that the Bible doesn't list the names of these heroes? Doesn't that seem a bit odd? After all, had they not been willing to lead in the front lines and boldly sing their praise songs, their enemies might not have heard them in the distance and become confused, therefore destroying themselves.

Today if a group of singers did something that heroic, they'd be interviewed on every morning talk show in America! We'd put them on a stage and ask them to tell their story and sing their songs again and again. Some record company would probably send them on tour, and groupies would almost certainly follow them everywhere.

I believe their names were omitted for a specific reason.

Make a list of all the famous prophets or preachers in the Bible. Then write down all the worship leaders in the Bible who were famous because they directed or played music.

The second list is quite a bit shorter, isn't it? By the way, if you wrote David's name, that doesn't count. True, he wrote many psalms, and he danced and played at least once that we know of. Still, other than playing the harp for Saul as a young man, there are no references to David ever leading music for a group of people. David gained notoriety as a great warrior and then as king. His psalms gained popularity as a result of the fame he already enjoyed.

In reality, the only "worship leader" who comes even remotely close to the fame and recognition of the preachers and prophets in the Bible is Asaph. And he was probably best known among spiritual leaders and those in his own peer group, particularly the Levites.

Preachers got a lot of recognition from both God and people, but musicians apparently didn't. Let's be really honest with each other now. Doesn't that bother you a little? I mean, after all, we do a lot of the work. Don't we get at least an honorable mention? Nope.

Here's why, as best I can see it: The more recognition and popularity we as musicians and worship leaders are showered with, the more difficult it is for us to point starry-eyed people away from us and to the Father. That is, in the end, the essence of worship, you know. By the very nature of our "business," we must help people fall in love with God and *only* God.

My Daily Praise

The Bible says, "Let the redeemed of the Lord say so, whom he hath redeemed from the hand of the enemy" (Psalm 107:2, KJV). Write down three statements you can tell someone else today that are reasons God should be lifted higher than yourself. Then, to practice, say them out loud right now.

{ JOURNAL

My Daily Surrender

Please don't leave this moment until you've settled whatever God has placed on your heart. Write a prayer, humbling yourself to solidify your heart's cry to be God's servant.

{ JOURNAL

Day 3: The Law of Divine Elevation

Do you love a good puzzle? Well, I've got one for you: What is the meaning of real success? There are countless books on library shelves that attempt to answer that age-old question. But even crime scene investigators, with their state-of-the-art techniques, would be hard-pressed to solve this one! Conventional investigation tools can't unravel the clues that will lead us to the truth. That's because *true* success does not come from following a clever method or by manipulating people and circumstances.

When I first surrendered to travel full time in music evangelism, one of the first things I did was buy a CD telling me how to get started in Christian music. In it, several leading artists shared their insights into how to "get discovered." (One suggestion that stands out in my memory was to go to Nashville and camp out on the doorsteps of recording companies!)

As good and practical as their ideas were, the advice that helped me most wasn't about what I should do; it was more about what I *shouldn't* do. Carman simply quoted Psalm 75:6-7: "For not from the east or from the west and not from the wilderness comes lifting up; but it is God who executes judgment, putting down one and lifting up another" (RSV). Carman said that our focus should be to go *deep* in our relationship with God and trust God to open the doors of opportunity he wants us to enter.

Of course, this advice goes against our human nature. We stubbornly want things to happen *our* way, in *our* time. Our carnal nature tells us we must scratch and claw and do whatever it takes to get to the top. But an often-used illustration sums it up well: How would it be to climb all the way up the ladder of success only to find at the top that your ladder is leaning against the wrong wall? That is why we must define and then settle for nothing less than *authentic* success (against the *best* wall!) in both our ministries and our lives.

It doesn't take much research to discover the secret to God's definition of success. In fact, the law of divine elevation is certainly *not* a mystery. Few principles get as much attention in God's Word.

Read James 4:10; Job 5:11; Luke 14:11; and Proverbs 3:34. All of these Scriptures point to one fact: We are not to be "the show." That honor is reserved for the Lord only. As John the Baptist said, Christ "must become greater," and we "must become less" (John 3:30). Yet, the promised result of our humbling ourselves is phenomenal: God will promote us! I know of nothing more profound for ministers through music—or any ministers, for that matter—to learn. Here's a good way to think of it: The law of gravity says, "What goes up must come down." The law of divine elevation says, "What comes *down* through humility will go *up* through Christ-like exaltation!"

But how can we know for sure that we would really prefer the success God would bring us to the prosperity, power, and popularity society offers? The clues are found in the seven little words from the second half of 1 Peter 5:6: "in due time he may exalt you" (RSV). These clues will point us to three reasons God's success strategy is far superior to the world's.

Three Clues That Verify True Success

Though I'm not a professional investigator, I've always heard that a good starting point is to ask probing questions. So to get to the bottom of why God's success is true success, let's start by asking, "Why would God elevate us?" To find the answer, we need to carefully examine the word *exalt*. How did God respond to Jesus' humbling of himself? Because Jesus willingly lowered himself and became a servant, "God exalted him to the highest place" (Philippians 2:9a).

The same Greek root word that is used for the word *exalted* in this verse in Philippians is also used in 1 Peter 5:6, where God says he will exalt *us*. The word includes the idea of elevating *above* others. In other words, those who humble themselves before him will receive the *same kind* of lifting up that Jesus experienced. The only difference is that he has, of course, been lifted up the *highest,* above *all* of us.

Understanding that God elevates us in the same manner he does his Son, we now need to ask another "why" question: Why did God elevate Christ? The answer is simple: to bring glory to himself. (See Philippians 2:11.) Obviously, therefore, God's intent in elevating us is the same as with his Son: to be glorified by our lives.

So now we have Clue 1: We are elevated in order to bring God glory. How is that evidence that God's success is best? Again, the answer is simple: We were created for God's glory. Therefore, glorifying him brings us the most fulfillment possible. You might say that God's success strategy comes with a huge tag that reads, "Complete *Satisfaction* Guaranteed"!

The next question we need to ask is *"How* are we elevated?" Our key verse (1 Peter 5:6) clearly says that *God* lifts us up. Yet how often do we run out of patience as we wait for his uplifting? We want to forgo his plan and manipulate our circumstances. However, for God to elevate us to our highest possible level, we must be faithful at each stage of experience and opportunity. We can't expect God to trust us with great responsibility down the road if we don't properly handle the small, "less significant" tasks he assigns to us everyday.

The Promotion of Asaph

As we discovered yesterday, worship leaders were rarely mentioned in the Bible. Asaph, however, was one exception. He was the most famous of the many worship leaders in those days. Each reference to him in the Old Testament shows his gradual elevation from virtual obscurity to national notoriety. He is the ideal example of how God elevates a minister.

Please take a few minutes to study the illustration showing Asaph's elevation.

Asaph's "Divine Elevation"

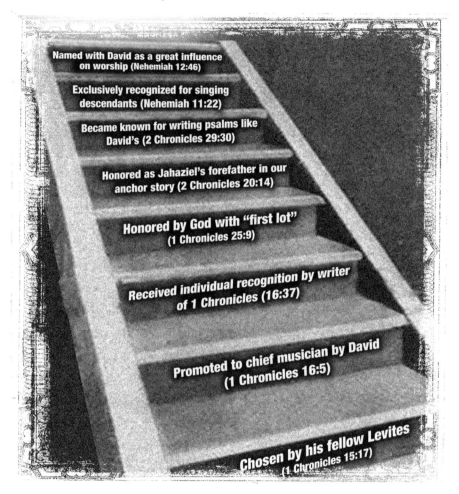

Named with David as a great influence on worship (Nehemiah 12:46)

Exclusively recognized for singing descendants (Nehemiah 11:22)

Became known for writing psalms like David's (2 Chronicles 29:30)

Honored as Jahaziel's forefather in our anchor story (2 Chronicles 20:14)

Honored by God with "first lot" (1 Chronicles 25:9)

Received individual recognition by writer of 1 Chronicles (16:37)

Promoted to chief musician by David (1 Chronicles 16:5)

Chosen by his fellow Levites (1 Chronicles 15:17)

If you were to carefully study every reference to Asaph, you would not find the slightest hint that he ever campaigned for any of his "promotions." Yet his fellow tribesmen took note of his godliness and skill and chose him from among the masses. God honored him as he remained faithful at each level of responsibility.

Throughout Asaph's story there is a strong sense of the sovereign hand of the Lord. And therein lies our second clue to true success: We are elevated by God's sovereign will. There is nothing more comforting than to know that omnipotent God exalted us to where we are. Such knowledge takes away the stress of feeling we have to fight to maintain our position. So we can now see that *true* success (God's way) not only brings us satisfaction, it also gives us *security*. (I'd say that smokes the world's definititon of success!)

But, for the really hard-to-convince investigator, there is still one more very compelling clue we need to examine. It answers the question "*When* are we elevated?" Clue 3: We are elevated in God's perfect time. First Peter 5:6 says God will exalt us "in due time."

Of all the clues, this might seem to be the most discouraging; in fact, "anticlimatic" might be a better way to describe it! After all, how could waiting and waiting for someone else to act (even if it is God) be a plus? I don't even like waiting in line at Wal-Mart! I sure don't want to wait around for weeks, months, even years while my hopes and dreams fade out of sight!

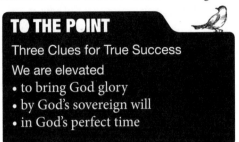

TO THE POINT

Three Clues for True Success

We are elevated
• to bring God glory
• by God's sovereign will
• in God's perfect time

Do you sense the fear, the impatience in those words? That's how the world feels; but we're not of the world. Our God has a plan for us; our every step is already determined by him. And in his good time, he'll raise us up as he sees fit. Clue 3 is huge because it brings us *serenity*. Rather than fretting about the future, we can focus on the present—on the awesome opportunities right before us *now*.

I recently helped at a crusade service at a local trailer park. No more than 50 or 60 attended. I added nothing to my résumé by being there that evening. So was I wasting my time? Hardly. I got to look into the eyes of two little boys who said they wanted Jesus in their hearts. I got to pray with them and see God's love pour all over them. I'm at perfect peace knowing God has me *exactly* where he wants—and I'm in no hurry to "move up"!

Here's a modern-day example that illustrates how and when God may choose to exalt us. The Christian music group Casting Crowns has enjoyed amazing popularity since its debut release. Lead singer and songwriter Mark Hall is also a full-time minister to students at a church outside Atlanta. To help teach biblical principles, for years Mark has written songs for his students to take home and listen to. One such CD of songs went home with a college student named Chase.

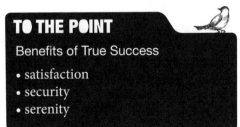

TO THE POINT

Benefits of True Success

• satisfaction
• security
• serenity

As Melanie Hall, Mark's wife, explained it to me, "Chase met Mark Miller, lead singer and frontman for Sawyer Brown, at a basketball camp, gave it to him, and asked him to listen to it. Mark Miller listened to the CD and loved it. Then one day in the spring of 2003, Mark Miller called my Mark and said that he had just gotten back from spring vacation with Steven Curtis Chapman and Terry Hemmings (soon-to-be-named

CEO of Provident Music Group), and he let them listen to the CD. They all agreed they needed to go together to make a CD with Casting Crowns. A month later we were in the studio." Millions of albums have now been sold, and the rest, as they say, is history.

We will not all receive the notoriety among our peers that Asaph did. We will not all hear the thunderous applause that Mark Hall does when he steps onto a stage. *True* success is not defined by human applause. And greatness is not determined by people's approval. Jesus said, "He who is least among you all—he is the greatest" (Luke 9:48). You and I will never be more exalted in God's eyes than when we are plain, ordinary *servants*—of the most high King.

Search your heart now. Ask the Lord to reveal any prideful motives and actions. Do you think yourself too good to perform certain tasks for others? Do you feel jealous or envious when others seem to prosper in their ministries more than you? Pray that God will form in you a servant's heart that is thankful for where he has placed you now. Decide to "bloom where you're planted." Express your meditations below.

JOURNAL }

Sing a hymn or praise chorus before the Lord right now. Praise him joyfully for his sovereign power and presence in your life today.

Day 4: Earning the Privilege to Lead

We've devoted the larger portion of this week on the essence of Christ-like leadership: a servant spirit and a humble heart. Last week in Day 4 we saw how indispensable being Spirit-filled is to spiritual leadership. Today I want us to concentrate on four other qualities that are necessary for us to be effective leaders of worship.

As the narrator of our story explains, "When [Jehoshaphat] had consulted with the people, he appointed singers unto the Lord…that should praise the beauty of holiness" (2 Chronicles 20:21a, KJV). Please notice the exact wording: "that *should* praise." Can we infer from this that there were some in Jerusalem that morning who should *not* praise? No, I don't think so. God loves to hear every one of his children praising him. I'm quite sure some of those soldiers joined right in with the song as they followed behind the choir.

However, while the soldiers were welcome to sing, they were not *expected* to sing and to praise. And therein lies the difference. The choir had been *appointed* by Jehoshaphat for a very specific task. In the same way, God places on us as worship leaders, musicians, and assistants a specific appointment or *calling*. I like to say, "You gotta know it." Paul *knew* he had a calling on his life when he wrote, "I thank Christ Jesus our Lord who has enabled me, because He counted me faithful, putting me into the ministry" (1 Timothy 1:12, NKJV). Charles Haddon Spurgeon said, "Let each man find out what God wants him to do, and then let him do it, or die in the attempt."[2]

You may be thinking, "I'm just a volunteer who enjoys praising the Lord. I never said I was 'called.' Besides, I thought a calling was just for professional ministers." Well, I'm not here to try to talk you into something. Only you and God know what he's gifted and anointed you to do in his kingdom. However, it is still true that long-term commitment and effectiveness in any area of ministry are sustained by a deep conviction that we are exactly where God has placed or appointed us. And that is not just for the "professionals."

The next quality of an effective worship leader drains the pool of prospects considerably. It is not enough that we *should* sing; the question is if we *would* sing. Just because God has called us to do something doesn't mean he will force us to do it. He will not. We've "gotta want it." In order to get off the bench and into the game, we need *passion*.

Ken Blanchard and legendary NFL coach Don Shula teamed up to write *The Little Book of Coaching*. Here's what they say about passion: "The best coaches and managers in the world are those who absolutely love what they're doing. The enjoyment of coaching is not a perk; it's an essential ingredient of winning. People want to see that passion in a leader."[3]

This doesn't apply only to football coaches. All who stand and lead others, especially in God's church, should show great passion for what they're doing. Darlene Zschech wrote about her praise team at Hillsong Church, "It doesn't work to have a team of people leading worship if they look zoned out. When you have people who are radical for Christ, and their joy is visible, it makes a difference in the church."[4] I love how Augustine of Hippo exhorted us to be passionate. He said, "The Christian should be an alleluia from head to foot!" The children of Judah certainly had reason to be passionate. They were literally singing as if their lives depended on it. Of course, we're not singing (or playing) to avoid death; we're singing to celebrate *life*. As the 18th-century Moravian church founder, Count Nikolaus von Zinzendorf, said, "I have one passion: it is He, He alone."[5]

Nehemiah is one of the most inspiring leaders in the Bible (and one of my personal favorites). When he heard that the Jerusalem walls were in ruins, he immediately responded like the passionate leader he was.

🐦 Please read the first chapter of Nehemiah, noting his passion for his city.

The third necessary quality that worship leaders must possess is discipline. We've seen who *should* sing: those who are called. We know that those who *would* sing are those with passion. This third characteristic narrows the prospects even more. Those with *discipline* are the people who *could* sing. Whether we play from a stage or push buttons in a control room, we must possess the skills necessary for the tasks. That only comes through *disciplining* ourselves to grow and learn.

"To…be the best," Ken Blanchard writes, "you have to push yourself…hard."[6] As Oswald Sanders explains in his book *Spiritual Leadership,* "Without this essential quality, all other gifts remain as dwarfs: they cannot grow…Before we can conquer the world, we must first conquer the self." Sanders goes on to lament: "Many who drop out of ministry are sufficiently gifted, but have large areas of life floating free from the Holy Spirit's control. Lazy and disorganized people never rise to true leadership."[7]

Webster's dictionary defines *discipline* as "training that corrects, molds, or perfects the mental faculties or moral character." The people of Judah were "in training" that day as they headed out, praising God's enduring mercy. They had certainly never done that before, so they were learning as they went. It's important to note that their determined *discipline* flowed out of their *passion,* which was stirred by their *calling.*

There is one more hugely important quality essential to effective leadership in the body of Christ: *integrity.* People with integrity are the ones who *get to* sing; they've *earned* the privilege to lift their voices or their instruments to the Lord. They're the respected saints who are *selected* to lead the sound crew or organize the choir music or assist the music staff. Another word for integrity is *completeness.* These rare and extraordinary Christians are complete, undivided within themselves. Based on Jehoshaphat's organized leadership style, I believe his appointments to the choir were quite deliberate. I believe only those whom Jehoshaphat *trusted* got the nod to go on this privileged mission, only those who were who they claimed to be, only those with *integrity.*

🐦 Please read 2 Timothy 2:20-21. Notice what kind of vessel or instrument God wants us to be.

Yesterday we read from Psalms that "it is God who executes judgment, putting down one and lifting up another" (Psalm 75:7, RSV). We focused on how God will lift us up if we humble ourselves. What we didn't consider was the other part of that psalm. While he's lifting up one, he's putting *down* another.

This is the part of God's nature that we would rather not think about. We like the fact that he "gives grace to the humble," but we don't want to dwell long on how he "opposes the proud" (James 4:6). Even so, there are many examples in God's Word where he does just that. David got a dose of the Lord's justice when his baby died. Jonah had a "whale of a tale" because he ran from God's will. Moses merely struck a rock when God had told him to speak to it,

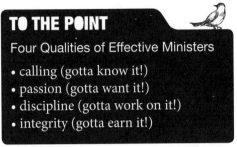

TO THE POINT

Four Qualities of Effective Ministers

- calling (gotta know it!)
- passion (gotta want it!)
- discipline (gotta work on it!)
- integrity (gotta earn it!)

and because of his disbelief and disobedience, he was denied entry into the very place he had labored toward for over 40 years, the Promised Land! (See Numbers 20:7-12.)

We have been bought with a price; we are not our own (1 Corinthians 6:19-20). The characteristics we've studied today are not optional components that may or may not come along later. The precious Savior who purchased us expects them to be "standard equipment" for us who are his children and ministers. "Therefore, since we are receiving a kingdom that cannot be shaken, let us be thankful, and so worship God acceptably with reverence and awe, for our 'God is a consuming fire' " (Hebrews 12:28-29).

My Daily Surrender

Review all four qualities we've discussed today. Ask the Lord to show you in which area you're strongest. Take time to rejoice over that! Now ask him to show you areas in which you've allowed yourself to slide. Claim his forgiveness. Write a prayer expressing your conversation with him. Jot down a specific action you will take today and/or this week to deliberately move you in the right direction.

JOURNAL

Think of three blessings God has given you that you have not thanked him for lately or ever. Write them below. Then enthusiastically proclaim the love and faithfulness he has shown you through these blessings.

JOURNAL }

Day 5: The Discipline of Difficulties

There is at least one more quality we must possess in order to be effective ministers: brokenness, which comes through difficulties.

In her book *Jesus, CEO*, Laurie Beth Jones tells the story of a meeting with some real estate developers. They had gathered to discuss a possible joint venture. Much to everyone's surprise the organizer of the group stood and began to describe in detail one of his greatest failures. One by one, each of the men revealed his less flattering side. When the youngest member was reluctant to share his mistake, the leader chided him, saying, "If you have not experienced failure, you cannot be a part of this group." Jones drew this conclusion from that leader's words: "If you have not been tested by fire, you do not know who you are. And if you do not know who you are, you cannot be a leader."[8]

In 2 Chronicles 20, Jehoshaphat and the children of Judah were certainly given the opportunity to discover "who they were." Of course, that was not the first time God's people had been tested by fire. Research any great Christian leader from the Bible or since, and you'll find the same pattern: Every one of them experienced deep and difficult trials.

For example, Larry Michael wrote of Charles Haddon Spurgeon, often called the prince of preachers, that he was "no stranger to suffering. Throughout his life and ministry, he suffered greatly as he ministered for Christ. The stresses and strains of ministry, the great expectations upon him week after week, the deadlines for writing, and the weight of spiritual responsibility—all contributed to the suffering he experienced."[9] Spurgeon himself wrote: "There is no escaping troubles. We are born into it as the sparks fly upward…Neither goodness, nor greatness can deliver you from affliction."[10]

Sam Cathy, an evangelist from Oklahoma, focused on affliction in a message I heard him preach years ago. It was titled "The Discipline of Difficulties."

In this sermon, Reverend Cathy shared an illustration about a rock tumbler. While on vacation in Arizona, he stopped at a rock shop. Standing at the counter, he noticed a banging noise coming from behind the cashier. Then he saw a small barrel rolling over and over. He asked the man behind the counter about the barrel. The man pointed Cathy's attention to several small stones lying on the counter. Some were rough and unattractive. Others were smooth, shiny, and beautiful. He explained that all the rocks were the same kind. What made their appearance so different was the tumbler. As he picked up a rough stone he said, "That barrel you see is tumbling a rock like this at this very moment. When the rock comes out it will look like this," and he picked up a beautiful, smooth stone.

Cathy, amazed at the difference, asked how the tumbler worked. The man said, "The rock remains in the tumbler until all the rough edges have been removed. The tumbler doesn't go too fast or else the rock will break. It doesn't spin too slowly, or the process will take too long. It rolls at exactly the proper speed according to the control of the master tumbler."

In John 15:1-3, *Master* Jesus speaks of his Father as a gardener who prunes the unwanted and unhealthy parts of our nature to make us more like him. Please read that passage now. Notice what we as "branches" are more able to do as a result of this pruning.

In the New Testament, fruit represents the products of our Christ-like lives (Matthew 7:16; Galatians 5:22-23). God's "pruning shears" are required to make us more and more fruitful for him.

My "Top Five" Trials

I have endured painful trials that have nonetheless eventually worked together for my good. (See Romans 8:28.) Please allow me to share a bit of "Dwayne Moore trivia" with you now. Indulge me as I open my closet of hurtful memories and let you peek in to what I rarely share with others.

Age 10—Three days after he had finished building a brand-new bakeshop for my mom, my father went to work and never came home again. He died of a massive heart attack, leaving my mother to raise me alone. God provided as we learned to lean on him for everything. He became my *Father* in the best sense (and my mom's Husband).

Age 13—I dedicated myself to the Lord, and soon the persecution began. My "friends" at school suddenly turned against me. They made fun of me, taunting me to curse or somehow mess up. I often ate lunch alone. It was during those days that I learned who my best *Friend* was (and still is).

Age 16—My home church had recently asked me to be its music director (something I did not want or ask for). After I had served there about nine months, a small group of noisemakers ganged up on me to the point that the deacons called a meeting with me. They didn't like my excitement level in the pulpit. I moved around too much for them, they said. It wasn't actually their concerns that hurt the most, but rather the way they unscripturally and ruthlessly went about attacking me and my integrity. That experience taught me that God is my *defense.*

Age 20—I took a part-time position at a church as minister through music while attending Samford University. Immediately after I started, a group of eight power-hungry people tried to get me to take their side against the pastor. When I refused, they decided to be against everything I tried to do from there on out. I shed many tears over how to respond in a Christ-like way to their tongue-lashings and behind-the-back tactics. It was during that year that God taught me how he is my *joy* even in times of trouble.

Age 21—Still reeling from the church trial, I began to notice I was losing my voice. After many lectures from my voice teacher and three different doctor's opinions, nodules were surgically removed from my vocal cords. I was a voice performance major on a special voice honors program; yet in my voice juries I could hardly whisper, much less sing. After surgery things got worse. The voice faculty finally told me I would have to change my major and leave music. That day I went out on a hillside and cried like a baby.

In time, God restored my voice, and I was able to finish my voice degree. And I have traveled and led worship thousands of times since. I have never forgotten what God taught me through that awful time. He showed me I had never handed over to him the treasure I valued most: my voice. God would settle for nothing less than all of me. I remember the moment on that hillside when I finally surrendered to him that which I thought was mine. What a sweet release!

Please read James 1:2-4. Note how many benefits we receive from the testing of our faith. I have found recounting my toughest trials to be an encouraging exercise. I think you will, too. After all, the more difficulties he has allowed *for* us, the more shaping he has done *of* us, and therefore, the more *potential* he apparently sees *in* us!

Look back now on your difficulties and be encouraged. Please take some time to analyze the most signficant trials you've faced. Answer the following questions regarding each one: (1) How long did it last or is it lasting? (2) What did you learn or are you learning about God, about others, and about yourself? (3) Did or does it serve to make you better or to make you bitter? (4) How are you using that trial for good, both now and in the future?

Every valley must have two mountains! Perhaps you've already found the mountain on the other side of your deep valley of trouble. Or maybe you are still so low that you are unable to see beyond your pain. It is true that some difficulties don't seem to end. How do we process those trials and turn them into victories? Paul prayed three times that God would remove his "thorn in the flesh." But the Lord said to him, "My grace is sufficient for you, for my power is made perfect in weakness" (2 Corinthians 12:8-9). Paul realized it was better to endure some suffering if it would ensure Christ's power in him.

Another story I heard Cathy tell was of a man who found a cocoon in his office. He set the cocoon on a shelf and waited for it to hatch. After a day or so, nothing had happened and the man grew impatient. He took a razor blade and slit the cocoon ever so carefully. Sure enough, within a few minutes, out came a beautiful Emperor Moth. As it spread its gorgeous wings, the gentleman waited for it to fly high into the air. But instead, the moth wandered over to the ledge and dropped off onto the floor. Distraught, he asked an entomologist why his prized moth couldn't fly. The insect expert explained that when the man slit the cocoon, he deprived the moth of the very struggle it needed to build strength in its wings. In fact, the expert said, the moth would *never* fly.

My Daily Praise

For every trial or struggle you recalled, write a sentence or two thanking God for the strength he built or is building into your "wings." Get on your knees, if you're physically able, and praise him for what he has taught you through your difficulties.

JOURNAL

My Daily Surrender

There's one final story from Sam Cathy's message that has had a profound effect on me. During a revival meeting, Cathy and the local pastor were invited to eat lunch with an elderly lady. During their visit, the woman told Cathy she wanted him to look at a picture she had of Daniel and the lions' den. She asked him to describe everything he saw in the picture. He described Daniel looking up at an opening above him from which rays of light flooded in. He pointed out that the lions were lying around Daniel with their mouths closed. After a couple of minutes, the wise old saint placed her hand on Cathy's shoulder and said, "What I want you to see is that Daniel doesn't have his eyes on the lions." Later he said, "At that moment I knew all hell couldn't defeat me." That lady had shown him the secret to true success.

Write a prayer completely surrendering your will to the Lord. Ask him to show you ways, gifts, or treasures you may be holding back from him. Surrendering them now could save you some painful pruning in the future.

JOURNAL }

1. Jack Hayford, et al., *Mastering Worship* (Portland, OR: Multnomah, 1990), 37.
2. C.H. Spurgeon, *An All-Round Ministry* (Carlisle, PA: The Banner of Truth Trust, 1978), 233.
3. Ken Blanchard and Don Shula, *The Little Book of Coaching* (New York: HarperCollins Publishers, 2001), 31.
4. Darlene Zschech, *Extravagant Worship* (Minneapolis, MN: Bethany House, 2002), 171.
5. J. Oswald Sanders, *Spiritual Leadership* (Chicago: Moody Press, 1994), 16.
6. Ken Blanchard and Don Shula, *The Little Book of Coaching,* 37.
7. J. Oswald Sanders, *Spiritual Leadership,* 52.
8. Laurie Beth Jones, *Jesus, CEO* (New York: Hyperion, 1995), 4-5.
9. Larry J. Michael, *Spurgeon on Leadership* (Grand Rapids, MI: Kregel Publications, 2003), 9.
10. Ibid.

THE MEANS

Day 1: It's Not About Style

A few years ago I was in Gatlinburg, Tennessee, on a Wednesday evening. I had been there all day looking for hotels our ministry might use for a conference we were planning. On that Wednesday night, I was faced with a choice: Stay in my hotel room (which is what I really wanted to do) or find a nearby church to attend. Sensing God's prompting to go, I reluctantly got ready and headed out.

As I drove around mountain backroads, I kept thinking, "With my luck, the church I find will be having its monthly business meeting tonight!" I finally came upon a little, white, picturesque church nestled against a hillside. Sure enough, as I walked through the door, I heard the pastor say, "We have a motion; do I hear second?" I immediately thought, "Great, I'm outta here!" Then the Holy Spirit's still small voice whispered, "Don't leave. This is right where I want you to be."

So I settled into a seat about three rows from the back. Scanning the room I couldn't help but notice that the sanctuary was packed with people—for a Wednesday night business meeting, no less! I was relieved when the business portion lasted only another 10 minutes or so. Then a guy, who I assumed was their music director, stood, holding a hymnbook. He asked for some singers to "Come on up and help" him. "Oh no," I thought, "it's been *years* since I've seen anyone do this." When I was growing up, I had often seen this "Y'all come" approach to leading songs. It was fairly common then among some of the small country churches to invite people—often unskilled and unrehearsed—to line up across the front and help "lead."

"I'm dreading this already," I grumbled to myself. Then they called out the hymn number of the first song. It was a conventional song that was no doubt written way before my time. I thought, "Yep, just as I suspected, their song selection is following right in line with their leadership style: old and outdated. Obviously these people are out of touch with how we do praise and worship nowadays. Somebody needs to 'enlighten' them about the new stuff that's out there." The service had not even started, and already I had decided I didn't like the songs they were going to sing or the leaders who were going to lead them. (Can you sense the spiritual *arrogance* that was just oozing out of me? Well, I didn't—at least, not yet.)

We'll come back to that story in a few minutes. But first I want to examine the prideful and stubborn mind-set that I had at that moment in Gatlinburg—which is, sadly, the same mind-set some members of our churches have, not just for a moment or two, but for their entire lives. As I sat in that church that evening, I obviously considered the newer songs to be superior to the older. However, for some of us, it's the opposite: Our opinion may be that the older worship songs and styles are actually better than the new. Either way, our prideful thinking remains the same: We assume that our way is the best way and perhaps the only *true* way to worship.

I recently read a book by a former worship leader who had left the contemporary Christian music (CCM) movement. His basic premise was that music with a beat is unscriptural. He said that "contemporaries" (as he called those who enjoy CCM) could never show scripturally why their music is appropriate. He kept saying he was going to back up his convictions with Bible references, but he never actually did! Every verse he alluded to dealt with motives of the heart, not with kinds of music.

I think it's time we take our assumptions to task. Like the gentleman who wrote that book, we too often assume ideas and beliefs that aren't really supported by God's Word. Francis Schaeffer wrote, "Let me say firmly that *there is no such thing as a godly style or an ungodly style. The more one tries to make such a distinction, the more confusing it becomes.*"[1]

I, too, could easily give you my *opinion* of what we should sing. But what good would my opinions do anyone? This is a *Bible* study. And the Bible simply makes no reference to a preferred style. In fact, not one of our modern music styles—country, rock, jazz, classical, R & B, and so on—was even around when the Bible was written!

So, if God's Word is apparently not concerned about style, why should we be so up in arms about it? If anything, the Scriptures seem to point to the importance of both the old *and* the new.

Please read and compare Psalm 96:1 and Jeremiah 6:16. Note any references to the old and the new you find in these two passages.

We're encouraged in these verses to sing new songs; yet we are also exhorted to seek the "ancient paths" when our ancestors walked with God. I have no doubt those "ancient paths" could include our ancestors' songs.

Now read Revelation 4:6-8. Examine the words the living creatures say in the last part of verse 8. Then read Isaiah 6:1-3 and note what the heavenly creatures sing in verse 3.

Did you notice how similar the creatures' song in Isaiah is to the four living creatures' song in Revelation? Together, those words could be two verses of the *same* song. I believe there's a good reason for this: Many scholars hold that the *heavenly* creatures Isaiah saw are also the *living* creatures John wrote about in

Revelation. Now consider this: These living creatures "never stop saying, 'Holy, holy, holy.'" What we apparently have here is an "old and traditional" song (so to speak). It's the same song they were singing in Isaiah's time, and they will still be singing it at the end of the ages.

Let's take a close look at Revelation 5:8-10. Amazingly, the four living creatures' *new* song complemented the old song they had just sung. Imagine that. Revelation 4 and 5 record the most powerful worship service in the entire Bible, and it's what some might call a blended service of both the old *and* the new!

Style is *not* the issue with God. He loves all kinds of music—as long as it honors him. What matters is not so much what we sing, but *how* we sing it. He wants to see that our music is flowing from hearts that truly worship him.

Have you ever stopped to think that classic songs like "How Great Thou Art" and "Amazing Grace" were new songs at one point? And some of the choruses that are so new to us now will one day be the old and familiar hymns of the next generation. The status of a song changes with time. The key to a good praise song is not whether it's old or new—or fast or slow, for that matter—but whether it expresses *truth* that Christians' hearts long to sing.

Now, back to that night in rural Gatlinburg. As the song leaders began the first song, I noticed about 50 teenagers in the front rows of the church. Initially I thought, "I really feel sorry for them. There is no way they're going to like this music." But to my surprise, they all picked up hymnbooks and joined in the singing. As they sang those old songs, several of the students started raising their hands in praise, and their voices grew louder and louder. A few even began to cry. It didn't matter to them that these weren't the hippest songs with the coolest beat. Their focus wasn't on the *music*; it was on the *Lord*.

As I watched in amazement, I realized I had been wrong and judgmental. The people in that congregation weren't the ones who needed to learn something about praise and worship. I was. And to make sure I didn't later begin to doubt their sincerity, God led some of the students to invite me to dinner after the service. I have yet to find more friendly and hospitable Christians anywhere. They showed how much they loved God by the way they treated me, a total stranger. In a sentence, they proved that their worship was *real*.

Jehoshaphat and the children of Judah also chose an old, familiar psalm. (See Psalm 136:1 and 2 Chronicles 7:3.) However, I doubt the style of the song had much bearing on their choice. They could repeat that chorus again and again because it exalted their merciful Protector. It was the message, the *truth* of the song they were passionate about. That's the same passion I witnessed among those students in Gatlinburg. And that's the very same passion God looks for in us, regardless of our style of music.

This exercise may take a little preparation. Sometime today (or tomorrow at the latest) borrow a CD of Christian music you would normally never listen to. Be sure it's music you wouldn't purchase on your own. Listen to the CD when no one else is around. If you can't understand the words clearly, read the lyrics on the CD's insert booklet. Your goal is not to *like* the song's musical style; rather, your goal is to try your best (with God's help!) to worship him through the *words* of the songs. Please approach this exercise with an open mind and heart. There's no telling what God may teach you through it!

Some well-meaning people of God have felt so passionately for so long about a certain kind of music that for them it's become more than a mere opinion; for them it's a conviction, a dearly held value and belief. They sincerely believe that their choice of songs and song styles is what pleases God the most.

Ask God to search your heart right now. When you see people praising God in a style of music you dislike, do you automatically think they couldn't *really* be worshipping the Lord through that song? Do you feel somehow that God isn't as pleased with their worship as he is with yours? Which of your opinions is God showing you through his written Word that you should change?

JOURNAL }

Day 2: It Is About Sensitivity

The other day while I was jogging in Mobile, Alabama, I ran past a large Baptist church. Its beautiful chimes were ringing out an old familiar hymn. About that time, on the opposite side of me, a jacked-up car blaring hip-hop bass beats pulled up to the stoplight. Talking about stereophonic confusion! I didn't know whether I should "bust a move" or find a quiet place to meditate! As bizarre as that moment was, it was a poignant reminder that we live in a world full of musical differences.

Studies have shown that only about 11 percent of new church members are attracted to a church because of its music.[2] George Barna concludes that, "For all the complaining that is lodged against church music, people may be more accepting or flexible than they let on." He based that opinion on his findings that 76 percent of attenders said they would not change churches if the style of music changed.[3]

Nonetheless, try explaining those statistics to someone who likes only Southern gospel music as she sits in her pew enduring a Christian rock song! Try convincing a classical music fan that music style isn't important as he squeamishly attempts to worship through a country "hoedown" version of "How Firm a Foundation"! The fact is, people are very opinionated about what they want to hear and sing. Anyone who's ever been involved with a church music ministry knows just how true this is. For example, what seasoned sound technician hasn't had someone approach the sound booth and insist that, for the pre-service music, they play "something more suitable for our church"?

Too many of us worshippers and worship leaders are quick to write off people who make such seemingly selfish requests. Indeed, we often feel quite justified in ignoring those folks. "What they are really saying," we remind ourselves, "is 'Play something that my group of friends and I will enjoy.'" Our response to them *sounds* spiritual enough: "But these songs lift up the Lord, so it doesn't really matter what you and your friends or anybody else thinks about them."

Well, yes and no. As we saw yesterday, any song that honors God and is scripturally accurate is, in fact, suitable to be sung at church. However, not every song is suitable every *time* the church gathers. That is because of a thing called *sensitivity*.

Speaking of being sensitive, stop right now, and breathe a prayer of praise and thanksgiving. Then ask the Father to make your heart pliable and teachable as the Holy Spirit reveals his Word to you today.

While particular music styles should not become a personal issue with us, we still need to consider them. We've already established that the *kind* of God-honoring music we sing and play does not determine our vertical relationship with God and how he responds to us. On the other hand, the music we choose may have an adverse effect on our horizontal relationships with others. And, as we will study today, the way we treat each other *does* ultimately affect how we relate to and please our Lord.

Please read John 13:34-35 and Romans 12:10. How do these verses encourage us to act toward other Christians? Are we willing to put aside our personal preferences and agendas and focus instead on ministering to the people around us?

Why is it that we want to force our music on other Christians just because we like it? Who is it we apparently love the most: them or ourselves?

(It's important to note here that specialized praise times are healthy and valuable for the body of Christ. Those meetings can and should focus on the specific music preferences of the particular group gathered for worship, whether it comprises teenagers, women, senior adults, and so on. Also, some churches have purposefully chosen to reach a more narrowly defined population group. When those congregations come together for corporate worship, the members expect the songs to be of a certain music style. That's not being unloving—that's being strategic about reaching the unchurched around them!)

Please understand this important point: In this lesson I'm not speaking of using music as a tool for evangelism—although it certainly can be that. We're not considering Christian music vs. secular. Furthermore, we're not evaluating specialized praise gatherings. Rather, our focus is on respecting one another in the *entire* family of God.

And in this spiritual family there are all types of musical interests. I heard about one pastor who used an ingenious illustration to help his congregation appreciate their different musical preferences. During a Sunday morning message, he asked people who enjoyed eating liver and onions to raise their hands. A few people raised their hands. Then he posed another question: "Who *doesn't* like liver and onions?" The sanctuary was awash in a sea of hands. He then compared eating that *vile* food—at least, according to my taste buds!—with liking certain songs. "We all have different tastes in music, just as we each have different tastes in food."

The problem is not in our varying tastes. Actually, that's a *blessing* God designed for his people! The trouble comes when we want to treat every worship service as if it's our own personal "tasting fair," and we're the judges. That way, if we don't particularly like a song, we can reject it and toss it out of the service. I don't think that's what Peter had in mind when he said, "All of you should be in agreement, understanding each other, loving each other as family, being kind and humble" (1 Peter 3:8, New Century Version).

Perhaps the key verse for this heart-of-God principle of *sensitivity* is Philippians 2:3-4. Please read that passage, and think about it in relation to music.

As long as the music of fellow Christians clearly and scripturally honors the Lord, we are compelled to honor them and their musical preferences. When we esteem others and consider them more important than ourselves, we are poised to let the world know we are Christians by our *love*.

Take a moment now to read the praise-inspiring lyrics of Psalm 27. Try making up a melody and singing the first verse or two. Don't be so concerned with the style of your melody. Determine instead to simply lift your heart to our "light" and our "salvation."

George Barna gave this sad summary during a conference on worship at Baylor University: "Everything in Worshipland is not OK," he lamented. Although many facets of worship have changed in recent decades, worship is still "primarily something we do for ourselves."[4]

Search your heart right now. Why do you worship? Is your real motive to bless your God, or is it to be blessed? One strong indicator is whether you can lay aside your own musical tastes and choose to worship the Lord with your fellow brothers and sisters, even when it's not through your preferred style of music. In the space below, write what God has shown you today and your response to him.

JOURNAL

Day 3: It's Even More About Substance

Wouldn't it be convenient if we could just run down to the local Christian bookstore and purchase a CD entitled *The Songs of Jesus*? These would be songs that Jesus himself recorded while he was on earth. That way, anytime we need to be reminded of what Christian music should sound like, we could simply pop in that CD. We would have before us a clear standard to follow.

Of course, there's no such recording. And as we've already studied, when it comes to the musical notes we sing and play, there is no such biblical standard. Because God has not laid down clear guidelines regarding musical style, we can be somewhat flexible with the kinds of music we use to praise him, and we can be sensitive to other Christians' preferences.

However, while this is true regarding the notes and beats of our worship songs, it's not at all true of the lyrics. For those, God *has* given us a standard. It's the most clear and biblical standard of all: the Bible itself. When it comes to what the words of worship songs should represent, we have no room to waver based on people's opinions and preferences. The truth of God's Word is not negotiable.

🐦 Please read God's words to Joshua in Joshua 1:7.

Soon after my father passed away, I began singing a song called "Now There's One More Angel in the Choir." I liked that song. I was comforted thinking of my dad as an angel who was now in heaven. And based on their compliments, other people who heard me sing the song enjoyed it, too. Then one day some- one posed this question to me: "When people die, do they become angels in heaven?" My first thought was "I don't know. How should I know? I'm only 12! Anyway, don't mess with my song. I like it." But then, the Lord's still small voice said, "Yes, but you can't sing something that's not scriptural."

So I did some research. And guess what. I had to stop singing that song because it wasn't biblically accurate. An evangelist friend told me he refuses to sing a chorus called "Hungry for More of You." He says it's not biblical. We don't need *more* of him. We already have all of him. What we need is less of *us*.

You might say, "That's too picky. It doesn't really matter that much." On the contrary, biblical accuracy in our music matters a *lot* to God.

Elements of Biblical Worship

Let's look at what Jesus had to say about worship. The Gospels record three instances in which he taught specifically about this topic. From these three short statements, we get a clear picture of what *God* requires in our worship and, thus, in our worship *music*.

To get an overall view of Jesus' comments on worship, let's first read all three passages back to back.

🐦 Please read Luke 4:5-8, in which Satan tempts Jesus after Jesus has spent 40 days in the wilderness. What did Satan want Jesus to do?

🐦 Now read Matthew 15:1-9. How did Jesus describe the Pharisees' hearts in verse 8?

🐦 Now turn to John 4:21-24, and read what Jesus said to the Samaritan woman about worship. What kind of worshippers does the Father seek?

The common theme in all three passages is that true, biblical worship springs from hearts that are fully surrendered to God. Worship is, first of all, a matter of the *heart*. That's why we learned in our very first week together that the essence of worship is to "Love the Lord your God with all your heart and with all your soul and with all your strength" (Deuteronomy 6:5). One might think of the heart as the *fountain* of our worship, and the songs we sing express the love that is flowing from our heart.

But is a pure and passionate heart all that is required for our worship to be acceptable to God? I believe we will find the answer to be no. To see what else is essential, we need to examine Jesus' words even more carefully.

According to the passages we just read, we must *focus* our worship not on just any god; our attention and adoration must be on the true and living God, God who is Spirit, the God of the Bible. When our understanding and concept of God become distorted, we are no longer worshipping the true God. Likewise, when the words of our praise songs do not represent the Lord as he revealed himself in Scripture, then we are not really singing to him but rather to a "golden calf" of our own making. (See Exodus 32.)

Jesus' words reveal one more requirement regarding the substance of our worship. Not only must we correctly represent who God is, but any worship that flows from our lips and our lives must also properly represent what God says.

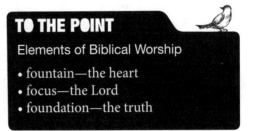

TO THE POINT

Elements of Biblical Worship

• fountain—the heart
• focus—the Lord
• foundation—the truth

Please reread Matthew 15:1-9. Basically Jesus stated this about the Pharisees' teaching: God had said one thing, and they were saying something else. They were *mis*representing God's Word. Jesus, therefore, called their worship a farce because they replaced God's commands with their own man-made laws. They were not worshipping God in truth, and it is truth that must be the *foundation* of all our worship.

By the same token, we must be sure that the contents of our songs and testimonies of worship are just as correct before the Lord as are the hearts from which they flow. The bottom line is this: If we don't follow God's precepts in everything we say and do, then we are not true worshippers of God. In the same way, if our lyrics do not represent accurate, biblical truth, then our songs are not true *worship* songs.

Let's put the children of Judah's song in 2 Chronicles 20:21 to the test to see if it qualifies as a biblical and acceptable worship song to God.

1. Did their song reflect worshipful hearts?

2. Did their song accurately represent God?

3. Did their song correctly represent what God has said in his Word?

Clearly, the praise song the people of Judah sang is an excellent example of the kind of worship song that honors and pleases the Lord. God's ultimate desire for us is to reclaim us from the bondage of our sin. In that awesome truth, we can all find hope. The Bible has many wonderful themes to draw upon in our songs of worship. But all praise songs should have one thing in common: hope. That is why I encourage you to examine all the songs you sing at church to be sure they are songs of the *redeemed!*

Of course, people who are *not* redeemed cannot truly appreciate or understand our worship songs. Some of the most satisfying themes of the Christian faith, some of our greatest reasons to praise, may actually turn off those who haven't accepted Christ. I once read an article by a worship leader who believed that "hymns and choruses which include the word *blood* are no longer suitable and should not be sung" in worship gatherings. His reasoning was that the "antiquated" term confuses and frightens younger generations who weren't raised in the church.

While I agree that certain "churchy words" need to be explained or updated, biblical principles and themes—like the washing of our sins in Christ's blood—cannot be improved upon. We must keep in mind that Christ's death on the cross can be offensive (see 1 Corinthians 1:23); therefore, our songs and lyrics will, at times, also be offensive. Some songs simply will not seem suitable, no matter how hard we try to be sensitive.

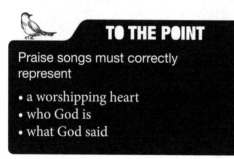

TO THE POINT

Praise songs must correctly represent

- a worshipping heart
- who God is
- what God said

Darlene Zschech has composed several well-known praise choruses, including "Shout to the Lord." She summed up the goal of our worship music like this: "A passion for our songs to be pure in spirit and truth must remain whether a song is to be *sung to thousands* or to a *divine audience* of One…I search for songs that bring…something straight from the Father's heart."[5]

We worship the Father, his Son, and the Holy Spirit. That's to whom we sing. That's about whom we sing. And whether we sing the songs, play them, write them, or just go down the road listening to them, let's be sure they properly represent the Lord and are worthy to be sung straight *to* the Father's heart.

My Daily Praise

If you can, listen to the words of one of the songs on a praise CD right now. (Another option is to sing a worship song that comes to mind.) Does the song properly express who God is and what he has said in his written Word? Are the lyrics words that your heart longs to say to God? If so, consider jotting down the verse or chorus lyrics of the song. Now plan to sing and meditate on those words again and again throughout your day. And whatever you do today, be sure to "praise the Lord, for his mercy endures forever"!

Think of the music you listen to most often. Are they songs that feed your spirit and encourage your walk with God? Are they biblically based? Or do the lyrics include ideas and concepts that are foreign to the teachings of the Bible? Take some time now before God to review your personal repertoire of songs. What can stay, and what should go?

{ JOURNAL

Day 4: Creativity Is the Door

This lesson fits perfectly in this week's study of the tools we use to praise God. Every day someone invents a new and needed utensil, perhaps for the kitchen or the workplace. And every day someone comes up with a way to improve an existing tool. Progress through creativity is a good thing in the world of tools. Case in point: The wheel was a fantastic invention, but aren't you glad that inventors didn't *stop* with just the wheel? In the same way, God has given us the wonderful gift of creativity through which we can make our praise even more powerful and effective.

God not only accepts creative praise from his creation, he enthusiastically *welcomes* it. Creativity is the passage through which we discover new and exciting methods to lift our hearts to God. A commitment to innovation is the reason new songs are written, old songs are rearranged, new technologies are tried, and fresh ideas are implemented.

Reasons for Creative Praise

I believe there are at least five reasons in God's Word for us to offer creative praise.

First, we should be creative in our praise because God is creative. His creative nature is described or inferred some 55 times in the Bible. Please read Genesis 1:1–2:4. As you read, note how many times the words *created, made,* and *make* are used.

To see the awesome creative genius of God, all one needs do is look up on a starry night or gaze at the full spectrum of colors in a sunset. How true that the heavens declare the glory—and thus the creativity—of God (Psalm 19:1).

Apparently, though, the Lord was not content with creating things only in the past. 🐦 Please read Isaiah 65:17 and Psalm 51:10. These verses show us that he continues to create both now and in the future!

Genesis 1:27 says we are all created in God's image; therefore, all of mankind has the potential to embody to some degree godlike characteristics such as love, mercy, justice, and faithfulness. And since God's personal nature includes creativity, every man, woman, and child is by nature also somewhat creative.

However, Christians who have God, the Holy Spirit, living inside them and flowing out through them should reflect even more of God's qualities. Christians have the capacity to be more creative than our nonbelieving counterparts. God, the ultimate and original creator, actually creates *through* us, his children.

Nancy Beach, in her fascinating book *One Hour on Sunday,* explains our source of creativity like this: "We are limited human beings who often wrestle with voices that say there are no more ideas and we can't create. But we serve a God who is the Master Designer…He has no limits, no creative end, no roadblocks. We have access to the Creator of All. For reasons I don't understand, he chooses to whisper ideas to the listening ones…if only we'll believe it and receive."[6]

🐦 Please stop right now and say this out loud: "I am creative because God who lives in me is creative!" Please say it again—this time with even more conviction.

Clearly God *wants* us to be creative in our praise to him, and our anchor story illustrates this. There's something very significant about what God *didn't* say through Jahaziel.

🐦 Please read 2 Chronicles 20:14-17. With those instructions to the children of Judah fresh in your mind, skip down to verses 21 and 22. Carefully compare what God said with what the people actually did. Did you notice a significant dissimilarity between God's directions and their actions? Once you see this difference, it will be glaringly obvious to you.

God never prescribed the praise the people of Judah lifted up. He never told them the exact songs they should sing. In fact, we have no record that he even told them to sing at all. Apparently that was Jehoshaphat's idea. They took some "poetic license" and came up with the praise thing on their own! God obviously approved of their creativity in praise because he blessed them not only with victory but with abundant spoils.

God gave them a directive: "Go out and face them tomorrow." He also gave them plenty of reasons to praise and thank him: "The battle is not yours." In a word, he set parameters and opportunities in place for them. And within those parameters he gave them all the freedom they needed to create an awesome, fresh, and encouraging worship experience.

Please read Colossians 3:16 and Ephesians 5:19. It seems Paul is giving Christians great freedom to express ourselves and create new songs of worship. Of course, the key condition for all of our songs is that they be Spirit led.

There's at least one more reason why we should be "pioneers" in praise: Creative praise captures the attention of others. Pastor Ed Young wisely wrote, "When people hear the same thing over and over in the same way, they stop listening. Failure is doing the same thing the same way and expecting unique results."[7]

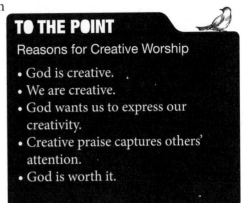

TO THE POINT

Reasons for Creative Worship

- God is creative.
- We are creative.
- God wants us to express our creativity.
- Creative praise captures others' attention.
- God is worth it.

Failure is not an option for us as worshippers and worship leaders. We have what it takes to succeed, to progress, to influence this world, and to bless our God. We have creativity. But this question still remains: Will we stand here outside the "door" merely gazing at it, or will we now boldly step through it and create something for God's glory?

My Daily Praise

Let's get creative! Write a short poem to God. You may not be a poet. It may take some brain power and good, old-fashioned effort, but it will be worth it when you catch a glimpse of what awaits you on the other side of that threshold. Don't worry about what it will sound like. Only you and God will know about it anyway, and I assure you he will love it (no matter how funny it may sound to you)!

Step 1: Pray. Ask God to give you creative thoughts right now.

Step 2: Brainstorm. Write down key words that come to your mind about God, about who he is or what he's done. Whatever's on your heart, put it down.

Step 3: Write a rough draft. Keep your poem to four lines if possible. Try to make it rhyme if you can; but more important, make sure it flows from your heart.

Step 4: Write it. Finishing something is always harder than starting it. Determination is required. You may have to scrap your first idea or two. But keep with it. I think you'll be pleased with your final product!

Being creative sometimes means doing strange and out of the ordinary things. Paul and Silas found a strange place to worship God when they sang praises in prison (Acts 16:25). An immoral woman did something daring, a way to worship that had never been done before: She wiped her Savior's feet with her hair then anointed them with perfume (Luke 7:37-38). These people offered ground-breaking praise for the greatest reason of all: Their Lord was worth it. And that's a powerful reason for *us* to give him creative praise: Our Lord is worth it!

How open have you been to new ideas? What's your first response when you see someone try something new at church? When was the last time *you* did something "strange" or unique, something *creative* for your most worthy Lord?

JOURNAL }

Day 5: Cooperation Is the Key

The State of Religion Atlas reports that there are as many as 20,000 Christian denominations.[8] Those numbers represent a lot of people who disagree with each other.

According to a report by the Hartford Seminary, there were an estimated 325,000 houses of worship in the U.S. in 2000.[9] I wonder how many of them started as a result of splits caused by people who couldn't get along.

Several years ago Paul Basden identified five styles of worship in American congregations: liturgical, traditional, revivalist, praise and worship, and seeker.[10] (Now we might also include postmodern in that list.) Every one of these styles is distinct and vastly different from the others—as distinct and diverse as the people who practice them.

In his book, *America's Worship Wars,* Terry York contends that a war over worship in the church started in the 1960s and continues today. The young people of the Jesus movement took their "wild music" to the streets. These individuals later became the pioneers of what York calls "the front." When the people of the front grew up, they wanted to bring their music and worship styles into the established church (which he describes as "the fort"). Over the years, champions of the front have clashed continually with people of the fort over what music and worship styles are appropriate. As York explains, "Agendas in worship are divisive. People are willing to go to war over agendas that have become heart-deep beliefs and convictions."[11]

Let's face it: Christians don't have a great reputation for cooperating with one another. We're often suspicious of how the people down the street worship. We don't easily allow new ideas and methods of praise.

I'm not implying that a mulitiplicity of denominations is necessarily a bad thing. And I'm certainly not saying we shouldn't take a stand over doctrine, "rightly dividing the word of truth" (2 Timothy 2:15, KJV). Furthermore, I agree with Rick Warren that our worship styles say more about our diverse cultural backgrounds than our theology and that variety in our worship is enjoyable to God and healthy for the body of Christ.[12]

But imagine what people outside the church must think when they look at us. They don't see unity among God's people. Instead they see disagreements and distrust. I think they may see us more clearly than we see ourselves. We need to ask ourselves, "What's wrong with this picture?"

Some years ago I decided to try my hand at painting. I found a beautiful picture in an art book that I thought I could paint. When I finished it, I was fairly proud of my painting—until I compared it with the original. Then I saw some serious flaws and discrepancies in my version. Today I want us to see an original "picture" of what cooperation in the family of God should look like. Then perhaps we, too, can know if there's something wrong with our version.

To fully appreciate a portrait, we need to look at *all* of it. Please turn to 2 Chronicles 20. Let's read the entire story from verse 1 through verse 30. As you read, make a note of any statements or words that illustrate how the children of Judah cooperated with one another. (One example is how the people "came together" in verse 4.)

How many references did you find that shed light on their cooperative spirit? I identified at least 12.

Now let's inspect this picture even closer. These people had plenty of reasons to cooperate with each other. Just look at all they had in common.

The people of Judah had a
- common need—They all faced anihilation.
- common enemy—They all had three vast armies coming after them.
- common purpose—They had all come to seek God's help.
- common focus—They all waited for God to speak.
- common orders—They all heard from God through his prophet Jahaziel.

- common praise—They all fell down and worshipped.
- common goal—They all trusted God to defeat their enemies.
- common victory—They all enjoyed the spoils of their victory.
- common joy—They all had a huge celebration parade through Jerusalem.
- common worship place—They all went to the Temple.
- common Lord—They all worshipped the same God.
- common peace—They all ultimately enjoyed peace with one another and with the nations around them.

An outstanding modern image of healthy, God-honoring cooperation is the Promise Keepers. I'll never forget sitting in the Georgia Dome with 50,000 men from many different denominations. Looking around I saw a kaleidoscope of skin colors. Yet none of that mattered when we started to sing and praise together. It was truly a taste of heaven on earth.

Bill McCartney, who founded Promise Keepers, wrote, "God wants to bring Christian men together regardless of their ethnic origin, denominational background, or style of worship. There's only one criterion for this kind of unity: to love Jesus and be born of the Spirit of God."[13]

Becoming a Team

So what do *we* have in common with other followers of Christ? Let's revisit the common ground the children of Judah shared. For each facet of this common ground, ask yourself, "What do my friends and I have in common with other Christians?" Remember, other Christ followers come in all different ages and from many different backgrounds, denominations, races, cultures, and styles of worship!

You may simply write yes or no in the blanks, or you may fill in actual words that describe what you have in common. But please try to fill in *every* blank.

Christians in Our Church	Christians Everywhere
Common need	_____
Common enemy	_____
Common purpose	_____
Common focus	_____
Common orders	_____
Common praise	_____
Common goal	_____

Common victory	_____
Common joy	_____
Common worship place	_____
Common Lord	_____
Common peace	_____

This exercise should help foster a team spirit within us. God designed his people to work as a team. We can accomplish much more in his kingdom together than we can apart. And he expects us to love, respect, and encourage our teammates.

We want to foster an environment where people's creations can safely fail. As much as we try, not every idea is going to be a good one. Not every song, drama, or sharing of faith stories is going to be a home run. The best way to squelch people's creativity is to criticize the last bad idea they had or shoot down their latest one before it has had a chance to succeed. We often criticize Peter for sinking on his way to Jesus. But at least he got out of the boat!

What others do in the church should, of course, be checked for quality, effectiveness, and doctrinal accuracy. Cooperation does not mean that anything goes. In fact, there are four definite criteria for the tools we use in our worship services—whether they're songs, videos, dramas, or whatever. All four of these are evident in the praises the choir lifted up as the children of Judah marched toward victory. First, everything we do in a worship service should *exalt* the Lord. Second a worship service should *exhort* the church. Third, a praise service should *evangelize* the lost. And finally, a corporate worship time should *engage* the listeners—it should be interesting and well done.

Of all of the things the children of Judah had in common, there is one thing they did not share. They did not have a common *vote*. No one was given the opportunity to raise his or her hand and say, "Uh, you know, I don't really like that song. Can we sing another one?" Or "Actually, those aren't the instructions I had in mind. I make a motion we search for *another* prophet to speak to us." Not only does cooperation not mean anything goes; it also doesn't mean everyone controls.

Author Marva J. Dawn wisely wrote, "It is impossible for our inner selves to be prepared to be open to God and receptive to God's Word until we silence our sinful selves—our efforts to be in control, to manipulate everything and everyone to accomplish our own purposes."[14] In *Life Together*, Dietrich Bonhoeffer made this selfless observation: "It is the voice of the Church that is heard in singing together. It is not you that sings, it is the Church that is singing, and you, as a member of the Church, may share in its song."[15]

My Daily Praise

Choose a song that your church enjoys singing together—a song you have the privilege to "share in." Sing it now to the Lord. Sing it from a *cooperative* heart.

My Daily Surrender

Take a moment to review what God has taught you this week. Now write a prayer surrendering your will regarding what God has shown you. Be specific as you write your responses to him.

JOURNAL }

1. Francis A. Schaeffer, *Art and the Bible* (Downers Grove, IL: InterVarsity Press, 1973), 76.
2. Thom S. Rainer, *Surprising Insights from the Unchurched* (Grand Rapids, MI: Zondervan, 2001), 56.
3. http://baptiststandard.com/2002/11_4/pages/waco_barna.html
4. Ibid.
5. Darlene Zschech, *Extravagant Worship* (Minneapolis, MN: Bethany House, 2002), 193.
6. Nancy Beach, *An Hour on Sunday* (Grand Rapids, MI: Zondervan, 2004), 183.
7. Edwin B. Young and C. Andrew Stanley, *Can We Do That?* (West Monroe, LA: Howard Publishing Co., 2002), 159.
8. Joanne O'Brien and Martin Palmer, *The State of Religion Atlas* (New York: Simon & Schuster, 1993), 98.
9. http://www.adherents.com/misc/FACT.html
10. Paul Basden, *The Worship Maze* (Downers Grove, IL: InterVarsity Press, 1999), 36.
11. Terry W. York, *America's Worship Wars* (Peabody, MA: Hendrickson Publishers, Inc., 2003), 15.
12. Rick Warren, *The Purpose-Driven Church* (Grand Rapids, MI: Zondervan Publishing House, 1995), 240.
13. Promise Keepers, *Seven Promises of a Promise Keeper* (Colorado Springs, CO: Focus on the Family Publishing, 1994), 161.
14. Marva J. Dawn, *Reaching Out without Dumbing Down* (Grand Rapids, MI: William B. Eerdmans Publishing Company, 1995), 265-266.
15. Dietrich Bonhoeffer, *Life Together* (San Francisco: Harper & Row, 1954), 61.

THE MISSION

Day 1: Impress Them

I realize I risk being misunderstood and written off as a heretic for insinuating—much less stating—that we are to *impress* people when we lead praise. I do admit I've had a difficult time sticking with this word, especially in light of what Warren Wiersbe wrote about trying to impress: "We minister publicly primarily to *express,* to share God's truth in sermon, song, and testimony; but we perform to *impress,* using our abilities to give people 'their money's worth' of enjoyment and entertainment."[1]

Ouch. That would definitely hurt if, by *impress,* I mean the same thing Wiersbe did. Fortunately, that's not at all what I mean, and performance for the pure sake of entertainment is not at all how or why any worship leader or team should seek to impress.

For too long the church has equated trying to impress with trying to dazzle people or seek glory and credit for ourselves. I certainly agree that we must be careful not to fall into that trap. When we hear thunderous applause at the end of one of our songs, it's easy to believe people are clapping for us. And perhaps at first they are. However, our responsibility as worshippers is to point people's attention *away* from us and toward the God who deserves all the attention and applause.

Let's consider the meaning of the word *impress.* Here are the first two definitions of the word in *The American Heritage Dictionary:*

1. to affect deeply or strongly in mind or feelings; influence in opinion.

2. to fix deeply or firmly on the mind or memory, as ideas, facts, etc.

Do you see how this can be a positive outcome for worship leaders? We *should* endeavor to deeply or strongly affect the minds and feelings of those we lead in praise.

We must distinguish between the act of worshipping God and the act of leading others in worship. While we know that God looks at our hearts, it's still true that people look at the outside. (See 1 Samuel 16:7.) We're (obviously) not leading God in worship; rather, we're leading *people*—humans with human eyes that can't and don't look past our exteriors. Therefore, our "outsides" must be considered. If people are turned off by what they see, we're not likely going to lead them very far.

I've noticed something as I've led thousands of students in worship over the years. Generally speaking, teenagers will give you about five minutes to get their attention. In those first 300 or so seconds, they will decide whether they want to listen and follow you. That may sound cold, but it's a reality that effective student worship leaders understand and embrace. And adults aren't much better. They may allow you to belt out one or two extra songs, but they, too, sum you up fairly quickly. Like teenagers, they'll either follow you enthusiastically or decide to "sit this one out." It really boils down to a good first impression.

Scores of people walk into our worship centers and sanctuaries every week with huge barriers to worship. Some are discouraged and defeated. Many are distracted by a plethora of activities. Some are disillusioned with religion and the church. Others are uninterested, even defiant about the idea of entering into a time of worship and praise. And there are always a few who are simply misdirected. These individuals tend to judge the service and the leaders based on their own ideas of how the worship and praise should be done.

With all those pre-existing barriers, doesn't it make sense not to give people yet another obstacle or hindrance? That is exactly why one of our priorities in leading praise must be to impress people strongly enough—not through our charisma, but by God's power—that they will *want* to follow us into God's presence.

To be sure you're clear about what I *don't* mean, please read 1 Corinthians 2:1-5 now. What do you think made Paul's words powerfully affect those who heard him? He was obviously not interested in performing or entertaining. Although Paul's words weren't eloquent or persuasive, would you agree that his presentation was nonetheless *impressive*? (Remember, *impress* means to "affect strongly" or "fix deeply or firmly on the mind or memory.")

Stephen provided another example of an impressive presentation in Acts 6. As he stood trial before the Sanhedrin, his judges "were not able to resist the wisdom and the Spirit by which he spoke" (Acts 6:10, NKJV). His words strongly *affected* them. His wisdom and anointing made an irresistible *impression* on them.

Both Paul and Stephen spoke with great wisdom that came from the Holy Spirit. They had obviously studied the Scriptures and invested much time alone with God to have such spiritual understanding and divine favor. They were neither sloppy, unprepared, nor apathetic; their passion and supernatural empowering *demanded* that people listen to them.

Like Paul and Stephen, the children of Judah displayed some fairly impressive characteristics.

Please read 2 Chronicles 20:18-22. As you read, try to imagine yourself as an onlooker. What did the people of Judah do that might have impressed you? Here's what impressed me:

1. Their humility and sincerity—They bowed and gave all glory to God. Even the most cynical of bystanders are often disarmed when we choose not to take any credit for ourselves.

2. Their passion and enthusiasm—Notice how they praised "with very loud voice" (verse 19b). Also, the way the Jadeite choir apparently did not even hesitate "as they began to sing and praise" on the front lines gives us a sense of their enthusiasm. No doubt many of the Israelites following behind the choir were strongly affected and influenced by their passion (i.e., they were impressed).

3. Their confidence—Jehoshaphat told them to have faith in the Lord their God and in his prophets (verse 20). They were completely confident that through him they would succeed.

4. Their excellence and preparation—Jehoshaphat told them what to sing as they began their march toward the Desert of Tekoa. It was a familiar song Jehoshaphat chose, so they most likely didn't need to practice it. They were already prepared and ready to sing. (We, too, need to be well prepared. People don't want to hear us practicing on them during the worship service.)

5. Their authority—These singers weren't the least bit timid about what they had to share. They knew that what they were singing was the absolute and undeniable truth that had come straight from God.

Reread the children of Judah's five impressive characteristics. Underline the one characteristic you believe you and your ministry are strongest in, and circle the one in which you are weakest.

There are exactly five priorities or goals we should have every time we stand to lead others in praise to the Lord. Impressing them is the very *lowest* of those five priorities that we will study this week. However, I trust we can all see why making our best first impression is nevertheless a priority for every worship leader, worship team, and praise band.

My Daily Praise

When is the last time you tried dancing before the Lord? Talk about something that requires crucifying our flesh. Our bodies despise looking silly, but David didn't mind looking undignified as he danced ahead of the procession that brought the ark! (See 1 Chronicles 15:25-29.) Go ahead; don't be concerned about looking impressive. No one's watching you but the Lord. Pray or sing to him as you dance. Don't hesitate. This is great praise practice!

Take time now to ask God to strengthen your determination to impress people for his glory. Pray now for yourself and for those in your church or band who help lead and facilitate praise. Ask God to empower your words and songs so that you may strongly affect those you seek to lead. Pray that their faith "might not rest on men's wisdom, but on God's power" (1 Corinthians 2:5). Be sure to write your prayer in the space below.

JOURNAL }

Day 2: Inspire Them

Perhaps you've noticed that the word *them* is listed at the end of every goal this week, and you're wondering why the word *God* isn't included in any of the titles. "I thought praise leaders were supposed to praise God, not focus on other people," you may be thinking.

Well, think of it like this: A football coach is in the stadium for the same reason the players and fans are: to play football. It really goes without saying that our main reason to be at church is to worship the Lord. It's absurd to think that worship leaders are not focused on worshipping God. That's like saying the football coach isn't focused on playing football! But what if the coach decided he was no longer interested in leading the players and all he wanted to do was get in the game and play? What if he ignored his responsibilities as the coach? The players would become confused and ineffective for lack of leadership, and the game would be lost.

We may see ourselves more as cheerleaders or band members than as coaches, but just the same, we all play a vital position in helping our "team" lift up powerful praise to the Lord. We must accept our role as leaders and embrace our responsibility to lead *them,* as we ourselves constantly strive to worship *him* with all that is in us.

Paul wanted us to understand the relationship our music should have between "them" and "him" when he wrote to the church at Ephesus. 🐦 Please read Ephesians 5:19. Notice to whom we are supposed to sing our songs. Some hold that singing to those in the congregation takes our focus off of singing to the Lord. But this passage seems to teach us that we can and should do *both.* Here's the key: A heart filled with gratitude and praise can produce some amazing music to God— music that overflows onto anyone listening as it makes its way up to the throne.

With that clarification and direction in mind, let's now turn our focus to the next of our five goals as we lead praise.

Music That Inspires

Few would disagree that music affects our entire being. It can lift our spirits and calm our nerves. In the words of William Congreve, "Musick has Charms to soothe a savage Breast, to soften Rocks, or bend a knotted Oak."[2] Even those in secular psychology recognize the tremendous benefits of music. According to an article in the Harvard Gazette, "No one can tell you how music therapy works. But there is overwhelming evidence that it does…The…successful use of music, in combination with other therapies [treats] Alzheimer's and Parkinson's diseases, depression, anxiety, chronic pain, pain of childbirth, autism, and other physical and mental problems including substance abuse."[3]

If music itself is so helpful, imagine how powerful, indeed *inspirational* it can be when God is involved. Webster's first definition of inspire is "to affect, guide, or arouse by divine influence." While just about any music can stir our emotions, only music that honors and extols God can actually *inspire* us, since true inspiration comes only from above. Martin Luther was speaking of God-honoring, inspirational music when he said, "Music is God's greatest gift. It has often so stimulated and stirred me that I felt the desire to preach…I place music next to theology and give it the highest praise."[4]

A great example of how music can inspire (or divinely influence) a person is found in 1 Samuel 16:14-23. 🐦 Please read that passage now. Notice in verse 17 that Saul only asked for someone who played *well.* But David's merely playing *well* would not have "caused the evil spirit to leave" Saul and give him relief (verse 23b). There was something much more important about David and his playing that actually chased away that "evil spirit."

Read the end of verse 18. Notice that Saul's servants realized God's Spirit had anointed David. Thus, when he played, in essence, the *Lord* encouraged Saul through David's music.

On our own the best we can do is stir up people's emotions. I do not mean to imply that showing emotion is bad. Watchman Nee points out that "the inner man needs emotion to express its life: it needs emotion to declare its love." But as he explains, "Emotion cools as well as stirs…When emotion arouses a man he is elated, but when it mollifies him he feels depressed…Before it is touched by God emotion follows its own whim."[5]

You see, our music may make people feel good for a little while, but unless God flows through our music and touches their spirits, the good feeling won't last. People get beat up by the world all week long, and they need genuine encouragement. As our music lifts up the Lord, the Lord will also lift them up. And what a privilege we have through our praise to "encourage one another and build each other up" (1 Thessalonians 5:11), I am currently discipling a middle-aged man who is a new Christian. He and his wife are separated, and he faces the very real possibility of having to raise his children alone. The other day as we met in my office, we began to list things we can do to help us in our walk with the Lord. We wrote down several activities such as "having a quiet time," "prayer," and "meditating on God's Word." In fact I thought we had covered it all pretty well. But then he spoke up and named one I wasn't expecting: "worship music." He explained, "Every time my girls and I start to feel down and discouraged, we turn on some praise music. It reminds us that God is still in charge and that everything's going to be OK." That man needed encouragement, and the Lord gave it to him through music that inspires!

My Daily Praise

Kneeling is one of the most powerful methods of praise. It helps deal a death blow to our fleshly nature! When was the last time you deliberately bowed your body before God in complete submission? If you are physically unable to bend your knees, then just bow as low as you can. Now with your head and heart bowed, raise your hands above your head and speak aloud to the Lord. Tell him how awesome he is. Tell him how much you adore and need him.

My Daily Surrender

As they headed out to meet their massive enemies, Judah's army must have been hugely encouraged when they heard the choir up ahead singing so robustly, "Give thanks to the Lord, for his love endures forever" (2 Chronicles 20:21).

Whether we stand in the congregation, sing in the choir, or play in the orchestra, let's keep in mind that there are people all around us who need hope, courage, and confidence. They need heartening, support, and fostering. The songs we sing with them could be the very catalyst they need to spur them on. And remember, they are not only listening, they're watching us as well. That's why it's so important that we offer a smile every time we lead.

Hebrews 3:13 says, "Encourage one another daily, as long as it is called Today, so that none of you may be hardened by sin's deceitfulness." How often do you encourage others—not just on stage but off? Are you more likely to offer a smile or turn away? Write a prayer surrendering to God.

JOURNAL

Day 3: Instruct Them

Which do you think is more important in leading praise and worship: instruction or inspiration, teaching people or uplifting them?

My natural tendency is to want everyone to be happy. Therefore, I tend to place the goal of inspiring people above teaching and admonishing them. However, a close inspection of God's Word has shown me once again that my natural tendencies cannot be trusted!

I know how challenging it can be to teach church folk—especially adults—new ideas and principles. We end up feeling sort of like Jethro from *The Beverly Hillbillies* when he tried to teach his dog, Duke, to fetch a stick. He'd throw the stick and say, "Fetch, Duke." Duke would lazily look over at the stick and then lay his head right back down. Jethro would go pick up the stick, bring it back, and throw it again. "Go fetch, Duke." But Duke wouldn't move. After Jethro had made several attempts, Uncle Jed, who had been watching Jethro exhaust himself, said, "Look, Duke's teaching Jethro to fetch!"

As challenging as it may be at times, we as Christians still have an obligation to try to pass on to others what God has taught us—whether we have the gift of teaching or not. One great way to do that is through our praise.

The Apostle Paul understood how effectively we can learn through music. Please read Colossians 3:16. Notice that Paul tells us to both teach and admonish through our songs.

Of Colossians 3:16 one commentator wrote: "Teaching and admonishing were to be present even in song. Song was to have another object than to please the ear. It was not for enjoyment, but for edification."[6]

Teach Them Through Praise

Let's turn our attention to the first kind of edification Paul talked about: teaching. *Please read Psalms 78:4-5; 145:3-5; and Isaiah 38:19. According to these passages, what can and should our praise of God do? *Now reread Colossians 3:16, and note what should dwell in us richly.

During Paul's time, the teachings of Christ were communicated orally because they had not yet been written down and circulated. It was vitally important that Christ's message spread, and Paul realized that one of the best ways to accomplish this was through songs. He was instructing the church at Colossae to sing songs that taught the doctrines of the faith. In fact, some of the most important doctrines were expressed in Christian hymns preserved for us now only in Paul's letters. Many scholars believe that passages such as Colossians 1:15-20 and Philippians 2:6-11 were actual hymns the early church sang that were adopted by Paul.[7]

Teach Them About Praise

Not only do we need to teach *through* our praise, we must also intentionally and continuously teach Christians *about* worship and praise.

When I was 15, I played and led my first song from the piano at our church. I remember my excitement as I started singing those familiar words "Amazing grace! How sweet the sound…" But when I looked across the congregation, only a handful seemed to share my jubilation. For the most part, I saw blank stares and bored faces. In fact some even had their arms crossed as though they were saying to me, "Bless me—I dare you."

Well, being the passionate worship leader I was, I took them up on their challenge. I sang the second verse a bit louder, but still they just sat there, staring. So I sang another verse and then another. The louder I got and the longer I went, the more obstinate they appeared to be. I got up from that piano feeling like a failure.

That day I complained to God, "Lord, I gave those people a great opportunity to praise, and they blew it. What's wrong with them anyway?" In God's gentle but firm way, he began to speak to my teenage heart. He revealed to me a valuable lesson: Some of the people in that room didn't participate more in the praise because there were important truths about worship and praise they didn't know.

*God led me to a verse that I want you to examine as well: John 8:32. Please read that powerful verse now. What did Jesus say would happen to us once we "know the truth"?

Some Christians aren't free to worship our awesome God simply because they don't know the *truth*. They are bound by traditions of worship styles or by confusion regarding why we worship and how we should worship. I believe another reason some Christians hold back is their fear of the unknown or a fear of what others might think of them. The Lord began to show me that I should not be angry with the people I sing to each week, as though they "should know better." Rather, as a leader of praise, my responsibility is to gently *guide* them toward what the Bible says about worship and to pray for them.

Admonish Them Through Praise

If you're not clear about what Paul meant by the word *admonish* in Colossians 3:16, consider this: Paul used the same Greek word, *noutheteo,* in this verse that he used when speaking to the Ephesian elders. He was concerned that they would be deceived by false teaching. "So be on your guard!" he told them. "Remember that for three years I never stopped warning each of you night and day with tears" (Acts 20:31). When we understand that *admonishing* or *warning* others through our praise takes precedence over encouraging and uplifting them, it will sometimes affect our choice of songs. For example, I was attending a conference a few years ago with some deacons from my church. One evening over dinner a couple of these guys began to talk about how they thought I should sing during one of the services that weekend. "You could really get those people fired up!" were the exact words one of them used. Sure enough, the next day they called me bright and early and said they had worked it out for me to sing in that morning service. "Sing something that'll get 'em shoutin'!" they insisted.

As much as I wanted to fulfill their expectations and as much as I enjoy lively services, I somehow knew in my spirit I was to sing an old song titled "Stirred but Not Changed." This song does anything but fire people up. The chorus goes like this: "I'm so tired of being stirred about the lost who need to hear. I'm so tired of being stirred that his coming is so near. I'm so tired of being stirred 'til I cry bitter tears. I'm so tired of being stirred but not being changed."[8]

As the song ended, rather than thunderous applause or loud "amens," there was complete silence in that huge room; no one even moved. It was obvious that God had something to say to us, and he used a simple song to convey the message. So let us never forget: Instruction over inspiration; that's the biblical priority.

In *To Know You More: Cultivating the Heart of the Worship Leader,* Andy Park devotes almost an entire chapter to worship leaders' ministry of teaching. He writes, "Every week, you *envision* people. You feed their minds...You confront them with truth...Remember, the worship you are hoping to foster goes far beyond the immediate reactions of people in a worship service. You are giving them food for thought, food for life."[9]

Please read Exodus 17:8-15. What Moses and the children of Israel learned that day was that the Lord is their banner of victory *(Jehovah-Nissi)*. God is our great rallying point to which we run in times of trouble! He will help us and save us. Praise your *Jehovah-Nissi* right now. Proclaim him as the banner of victory over you, your family, and your church.

God taught me another profound truth that morning years ago as I walked away from the piano frustrated that "those people didn't praise." This lesson was much more personal and painful. "Dwayne, the people in the pews aren't the only ones who need to know the truth about worship. You've got a lot to learn yourself. Don't you realize that when you were upset with them, you took your focus off *me*? At that moment you became just like some of them: You yourself stopped worshipping me."

How often do you get angry at others when it's really you who has the problem? In order for us to instruct others, Colossians 3:16 tells us that his Word must first dwell "richly" in us. How well does his Word dwell in you? Isaiah said, "The Sovereign Lord has given me an instructed tongue, to know the word that sustains the weary. He wakens me morning by morning, wakens my ear like one being taught" (Isaiah 50:4). How many mornings do you awake so you can hear him instruct *you* from his Word? Write a prayer of response below.

JOURNAL }

Day 4: Influence Them

J.I. Packer said this about the word *taste*: "To 'taste' is, as we say, to 'try' a mouthful of something, with a view to appreciating its flavor. A dish may look good, and be well recommended by the cook, but we do not know its real quality till we have tasted it."[10]

What passionate worshippers want more than anything is for other people to "try" God's goodness and to know him as we've experienced him. We yearn for others to "taste and see that the Lord is good" (Psalm 34:8a).

🐦 Please read Psalm 34:1-8. Underline each of David's statements that encourages others to join him in worshipping and experiencing the Lord.

When David said, "Glorifiy the Lord with me; let us exalt his name together" (verse 3), he expressed what should be the heart's cry of every church musician and worship assistant. We have each been entrusted to lead God's people in praise. As we've already learned, leadership is influence. Therefore, *influencing* other Christians to worship must be a very high priority for us.

In order for us to effectively influence others to come along with us in praising the Lord, we must first be sure that other, lower-priority goals are adequately met.

Hypothetical Joe

So far we've learned that our number five goal is to impress others, number four is to inspire them, and number three is to instruct them. To help illustrate how these goals work hand in hand, allow me to introduce you to Hypothetical Joe.

Joe has never been to your church before, but this morning he chose to try out your service. Joe is a young professional guy in his early 30s, successfully climbing the corporate ladder. He is a professing Christian with an off-and-on commitment to church. However, Joe knows little about the Bible and even less about biblical worship and praise.

Joe arrives a few minutes early to get a good seat. The first thing he notices is how sharp the program guide looks and how the screens up front are scrolling with announcements and creative quotes. He likes the atmosphere and makes a mental note that a detail-oriented person like himself obviously took a lot of deliberate care to create this environment. The praise band and choir start the service on time as they open with an upbeat song. Immediately, Joe begins to enjoy the energy and enthusiasm the choir exudes. They sound and look great. Joe is *impressed.*

When Joe walked in, he had no intention of singing along—it's just not his thing. And he was doing pretty well sticking to his plan until they started singing one particular song; it's an older hymn he's heard before. The choir and congregation are singing so loudly that it's contagious. When the music leader says, "Come on, let's all lift our voices together!" it seems like a personal invitation to Joe. He now finds himself sounding out some notes of his own. One might say he's been *inspired* to sing.

Joe has sung so much today that he has surprised himself. He can't remember ever having participated like this in a church service. He's never really known *why* people think they have to sing when they're at church. But now, he reasons that it must be because they have such a good time doing it. "Singing can be fun," Joe muses. But then a light bulb comes on in his mind. The music leader quotes a verse that Joe has never heard before: "Praise the Lord. Sing to the Lord a new song, his praise in the assembly of the saints" (Psalm 149:1). "OK," Joe almost says out loud, "now I get it. We're supposed to be singing to God. We should be talking to *him* when we sing." The very next song is a simple, repetitive chorus that addresses God directly. Joe closes his eyes and sings the words straight to God. He's never done that before. But he knows he will do it again. Why? He's now been *instructed* how to praise.

By the end of our music service, Joe has been effectively *influenced* to sing and praise God. His heart is warmed, and his mind is ready to hear God's Word. How did this happen? Simply put, the Holy Spirit worked through some human vessels to bring him to the point of true, biblical worship. Each "lesser" goal played an important part toward allowing the worship leaders to do what worship leaders should always try to do: *influence* others to "glorify the Lord" with them (Psalm 34:3).

Jehoshaphat's Example

Jehoshaphat was a great leader. He must have been, since he influenced the children of Judah to march unarmed right into the enemies' path! They followed his leadership because he patiently achieved every one of these goals.

Read 2 Chronicles 20:5-12. What about Jehoshaphat and his prayer do you think most likely made a favorable *impression* on the children of Judah?

Now read verses 14-17 of the same chapter. Note the *instruction* and admonition the children of Judah received through Jahaziel. Jehoshaphat desired that God instruct not only him, but also his people. God chose to speak through Jahaziel to give all of them the "game plan."

Look at verse 20. Notice the words of *inspiration* Jehoshaphat gave to the choir and army just before they went to meet their enemies. He basically gave them a pep talk. He fired them up, just as a coach would before a big game. They knew they should have faith; they just needed to hear it from their leader. The fact that they carried out his instructions precisely proves the *influence* he had earned over them. Now they not only *had* to follow Jehoshaphat; they *wanted* to.

John Maxwell has a favorite proverb about leadership that's worth memorizing: "He who thinketh he leadeth and hath no one following him is only taking a walk"![11]

Oh God, please make us true *influencers* in your kingdom.

My Daily Praise

As Jehoshaphat prayed in 2 Chronicles 20, he acknowledged three important attributes of God. This ultimately led him and the people of Judah to greater faith and profound joy. Take time to consider these three attributes right now. Write a prayer to God expressing your thankfulness for each. I like to call these steps the "Recipe for Rejoicing." Once you've completed this little exercise, I think you'll be rejoicing, too!

Thank you, God, for your faithfulness because

JOURNAL

Thank you, God, for your holiness because

JOURNAL

Thank you, Lord, for your enduring mercy because

JOURNAL

My Daily Surrender

According to Joshua 6, the people of Jericho had constructed a huge wall that prevented God's people from reaching them. In much the same way people have constructed seemingly insurmountable walls in their hearts and minds to prevent God from coming in and taking control. As worship leaders we cannot merely *express* the greatness and grace of our God to those in the congregation. What if the Israelites had settled for only looking at the wall, hoping it would somehow fall as they lifted praise to God with their trumpets and songs? The wall might never have fallen! No, they marched around that wall seven times. They were *determined* the wall would come down, and they trusted the Lord to honor their obedience to him.

How determined are you to influence those around you to worship? Are you content to just stand there, singing or playing? Do you feel it's their problem if they don't follow in praise to the Most High? Or do you sense a responsibility to help them *want* to follow? It was clearly God's power that brought the wall down that day in Jericho. But it was clearly God's *people* whom the Lord used to help it fall! Ask God to use you and your worship team to help bring down someone's "wall" this coming Sunday.

Day 5: Illumine Them

For years I couldn't quite understand why in 2 Chronicles 20:21b Jehoshaphat chose to sing, "Praise the Lord, for His mercy endures forever" (NKJV). I know this was a familiar doxology for them. But if Jehoshaphat could give them only one statement to repeat, why not make it something they could say straight to God? Why not sing "Praise *you*, Lord, for *your* mercy endures forever"? Maybe it's because Jehoshaphat and those singers wanted their praise to *influence* those who heard it. Based on what they were proclaiming, they obviously desired that everyone "praise the Lord."

How effective were they? Did they influence all those within earshot? Did, in fact, *everyone* praise the Lord because of their urging? Certainly some of those soldiers who followed chose to worship. Perhaps several who gathered watching them along the route were motivated to join them in praising their God. However, even though many did decide to worship, the answer to the question is still no. No, they didn't influence everyone. The enemy armies, for example, most certainly did not choose to worship Israel's God. When they heard the praise, rather than turning to God and giving thanks, they turned on each other! Despite their passionate plea, the children of Judah simply could not get everyone to follow them. The same is true of us. No leader will ever have a 100 percent following. That is precisely why *influence* can't be our primary goal as lead worshippers.

There are at least two reasons for this. First, we are setting ourselves up for failure. We will never lead everyone in the room to praise. The lost *can't* worship God, and some Christians simply *won't!* Second, when we make influencing people our top priority we give ourselves too much credit. When we believe it's our fault if they don't worship, we're really saying that we cause and control their praise. But the fact is, we're just not that good! That old saying holds true: "You can lead a horse to water, but you can't make him drink." And even if our motives are pure, would you really want that much responsibility?

Digging for Treasure

So what is our ultimate goal? What can we accomplish every single time we stand in front of others to lead praise and worship?

To begin to unearth the answer, let's read 2 Chronicles 20:21-29. Once the children of Judah returned from their "battle-less" battle, the other nations didn't necessarily fall down in repentance and begin to worship God when they heard the news. Even so, they were undeniably and directly affected by Judah's praise.

Please read 1 Peter 2:9. According to this verse, because we are God's chosen people, we are supposed to "declare the praises of him who called [us] out of darkness into his wonderful light." This is the *key* that unlocks a hidden treasure chest of wisdom for us as worshippers and worship leaders. Once we see that our ultimate responsibility is simply to declare God's praises to those around us, we are only a turn of the key away from clearly understanding our ultimate goal.

Now please read about a bold request Moses made of God in Exodus 33:12-23. Now read Exodus 34:27-30. When Moses returned, what was different about him?

It was obvious to all that Moses had been with God because he had the "glow that shows." In the same way it should be evident to others that we have been with the Lord. Worship leaders are not in show business; we are in the *glow* business. And people need to see us shining for God.

When the Sanhedrin court looked upon Stephen as he was being tried, they "saw that his face was like the face of an angel" (Acts 6:15). It was *evident* that Stephen had been in God's presence. When Peter and John stood before the Jewish council, the council was amazed that these "unschooled, ordinary men" were so bold. It was *evident* to them that Peter and John "had been with Jesus" (Acts 4:13).

True, we cannot force others into God's presence; however, like these men, we can always bring God's presence to *them*. Dan DeHaan put it like this:

> "Today we must do the same thing that Moses did. Those of us who are leaders must carry God's presence into the lives of people. Most of us do the opposite. We carry people into the presence of God. We must come down from His presence to minister with anointing from above."[12]

The Test of Illumination

How can we *know* if we've reached our highest goal when we stand to lead praise? How can we be sure that we've *illumined* those watching?

Return to 2 Chronicles 20, and carefully read verse 29. Did you notice that when the nations talked about who fought against Israel's enemies, they didn't talk about Judah and didn't give the Jadeites credit for the victory? They talked about the *Lord!* That's how we know that the people of Judah achieved their ultimate goal: God got all the praise in the end. The children of Judah *showed forth* his praises, and the world stood up and took notice—not of their great accomplishments, but of God's great power. When people are merely impressed, inspired, or instructed, they may leave talking about us. When they are influenced they may leave talking about how God *used* us to help them. But when they are *illumined,* they will be in such awe of God's glory and greatness that they may not even remember we were in the service.

Biblical worship is evangelistic, because worship that focuses on God will in turn point others to him. When we see a glimpse of his holiness, we get a startling and clear view of our own sinfulness. Sally Morgenthaler, in her book *Worship Evangelism*, writes, "The purpose or intent of worship is not evangelism…Yet, evangelism…should be one of worship's dimensions or by-products. Evangelism is the natural and expected fruit of worship that is authentic and full of God's presence and truth."[13] As his people, our praise should show forth the truth and character of the Lord so those around us "will see and fear and put their trust in the Lord" (Psalm 40:3).

I'll never forget what a fellow said to me a few years ago. He had picked me up at my hotel for a festival service in Plano, Texas. Driving there, he commented that he loved to sing in the choir; it's something he would always do. When I asked him why, he said he came to church for the first time as an adult. When he walked in the service, he was immediately drawn to the smiling faces and vibrant voices of the choir. He thought, "I want whatever they have." By the end of the worship time, he realized that what they had and what he needed was Jesus. He could hardly wait for the pastor to give the invitation so he could trust Christ as his Savior!

More than influencers, God expects us to be *illuminators.* More than to be leaders, he's called us to be a *light* in the darkness. In this we cannot and we *must* not fail.

My Daily Praise

Congratulations! We've reached the top of our mountain of learning! With a little determination and a lot of God's grace, we've scaled the heights! Don't think we're finished yet, though. There's one more profoundly important week to go.

Before we get into Week 9, take some time over the next couple of days to complete the "View From the Top" work sheet (pp. 144-145). If you're like me, you rarely take enough time to celebrate an accomplishment. The children of Judah were smarter than that: They took a full day to celebrate their victory (2 Chronicles 20:26). Even now, take a moment to thank God for helping you get this far in your journey. Go ahead. Use one of your newly discovered favorite ways to praise. I dare you!

There's an amazing surprise waiting for us once we reach the peak of our proverbial mountain. As much as I want to go ahead and point it out to you, I'd rather you first ask the Lord to give you wisdom to see it for yourself. But don't be too concerned. If he chooses to use me to help you discover it, I'm more than willing to oblige!

Take some time to write down what God has taught you today. Then ask him to grant you wisdom to see all he wants you to see from this elevated vantage point.

{JOURNAL

1. Warren W. Wiersbe, *Real Worship* (Grand Rapids, MI: Baker Books, 2000), 172.
2. William Congreve, *The Mourning Bride,* act 1, scene 1 (http://en.wikiquote.org/wiki/William_Congreve).
3. Harvard University Gazette, "Treating ills with music" (http://www.hno.harvard.edu/gazette/2000/11.09/01-music.html).
4. Ewald M. Plass, ed., *What Luther Says* (St. Louis, MO: Concordia Publishing House, 1959), 982, 980.
5. Watchman Nee, *The Spiritual* Man (New York: Christian Fellowship Publishers, Inc., 1968), 193, 200.
6. *People's New Testament,* Christian Classics Ethereal Library (http://www.ccel.org/ccel/johnson_bw/pnt.pnt1203.html?scrBook=Col&scrCh=3-3&scrV=1...)
7. *The NIV Study Bible* (Grand Rapids, MI: Zondervan Publishing House, 1995), 1819.
8. *Stirred But Not Changed*/Lanny Wolfe/Lanny Wolfe Music/ASCAP. All rights controlled by Gaither Copyright Management. Used by permission.
9. Andy Park, *To Know You More* (Downers Grove, IL: InterVarsity Press, 2002), 90.
10. J.I. Packer, *Knowing God* (Downers Grove, IL: InterVarsity Press, 1973), 39.
11. John C. Maxwell, *Developing the Leader in You* (Nashville, TN: Thomas Nelson Publishers, 1993), 1.
12. Dan DeHaan, *The God You Can Know* (Chicago: Moody Press, 1982), 32.
13. Sally Morgenthaler, *Worship Evangelism* (Grand Rapids, MI: Zondervan, 1999), 88.

THE VIEW FROM THE TOP

Here you stand on the top of a mountain of learning. You've grown in your understanding of praise and worship as you've made the climb these past several weeks. Take a good look around. Breathe the holy air; gaze for a while on the amazing grace of our God. Now jot down some ways you sense that your pure and more powerful praise to the Lord is having an impact.

How do you believe your praise has affected the Lord?

How do you sense your praise has affected your church?

How do you sense your praise has affected those around you?

How do you sense your praise has affected you, both spiritually and emotionally?

How has your praise affected your battles with temptations and struggles?

What week of this study has helped you the most? Why?

THE MAIN THING

Day 1: Keep Fighting

Today we find ourselves at the summit and face to face with this pressing question: What now? What did God bring us all the way up here to find? And what are we to do with all this new-found faith and instruction as worshippers of El Shaddai? What is, in fact, the main thing God wants for us?

Once again, our anchor story points toward the answer. Jehoshaphat and the people of Judah demonstrated what is most important for true worshippers of God.

Please read 2 Chronicles 20:26-27. After Jehoshaphat and the men of Judah celebrated in the Valley of Beracah, they returned to Jerusalem. They joyfully went *back* to the people they knew—and they shared with those folks the blessings God had given them.

What, ultimately, was God's goal when he communed with Moses on Mount Sinai and gave him the Law? What was Moses' responsibility once he had heard from the Lord? God made his intentions for Moses abundantly clear in Exodus 19:3: "Then Moses went up to God, and the Lord called to him from the mountain and said, 'This is what you are to say to the house of Jacob and what you are to tell the people of Israel.' " Moses had no choice but to go back down to the valley and share what he had learned. That was his *mission*.

As we stand firm now on the peak of our metaphorical mountain, take another look around. What do you see? Beyond the rocks and trees, there's a valley below, a valley filled with people. Those are the people Jesus died for. Those are the ones to whom we are called to minister, to love, to encourage, and to help lead in worshipping and experiencing our Lord. That is *our* mission.

I believe the greatest achievement of the people of Judah in 2 Chronicles 20 is that they completed their mission; they finished well. The greatest statement you or I can ever hope to hear is our heavenly Father saying, "Well done, good and faithful servant" (Matthew 25:21a, KJV).

Years ago, I wrote in my journal this goal for my life: "To say as Paul, 'I have fought the good fight, I have finished the race, and I have remained faithful' " (2 Timothy 4:7, NLT). Paul's "main thing" had always been to complete his earthly assignment. In his farewell address to the church leaders in Ephesus, he said, "What matters most to me is to finish what God started: the job the Master

Jesus gave me of letting everyone I meet know all about this incredibly extravagant generosity of God" (Acts 20:24b, *The Message*).

In the last letter he would ever pen, Paul revealed to Timothy five keys to finishing well: keep fighting, keep focused, keep faithful, keep fresh, and keep fruitful. All of these are absolute requirements if we are to let as many people as possible know about the generosity of God. Not surprisingly, every one of these keys is clearly evident as the children of Judah returned triumphantly to Jerusalem.

So tighten the laces of your hiking boots and secure your pack. Let's start heading back down. God still has some profound insights for us as we return.

Fight the Good Fight

The first principle we must employ if we are to finish well is to *keep fighting*.

"I could still hold my weapon. I could still walk. My legs weren't blown off. I wanted to finish the mission." That was Lance Cpl. Jaime M. Magallanes' attitude when he was wounded by an enemy sniper while on a patrol in Ar Ramadi, Iraq, March 23, 2003. Amazingly, the young warrior ignored his injury and turned his concerns toward his fellow Marines and their mission. "We wiped his wound down and dressed it," said a Navy lieutenant. "We also listened to his lungs to see if he was breathing fine. He was cool and calm and said he wanted to return to the fight."[1]

Well has it been said that all Christ followers must recognize that the Christian life is not a playground but a *battlefield* where conflicts are won and lost in real spiritual battles. No matter how difficult the fighting becomes for us, like Magallanes, as Chrisians we must never quit. Alfred Plummer observed that "Military service is either perpetual warfare or perpetual preparation for it…The soldier, so long as he remains in the service, can never say, 'I may lay aside my arms and my drill: all enemies are conquered: there will never be another war.'"[2]

Of course, the enemies we Christians are battling are not other people, especially not other Christians (although it may seem that way at times). There is nothing good that will come from waging war against each other in the family of God. The "good fight" Paul fought was one "against evil rulers and authorities of the unseen world, against mighty powers in this dark world, and against evil spirits in the heavenly places" (Ephesians 6:12b, NLT). When Paul said he had "fought the good fight," the Greek word he used for *fight* gives us the English word *agonize* and was used in military endeavors to describe the concentration, discipline, and extreme effort needed to win.[3]

For the follower of Christ, pressures and difficulties are inevitable. Jesus said, "In the world you will have tribulation; but be of good cheer, I have overcome the world" (John 16:33, NKJV). Charles Stanley wrote, "Somewhere we have gotten the erroneous idea that our ultimate goal as Christians is to come to a place in our lives where we are never tempted. Ironically, the very opposite is true. The more godly we become, the more of a threat we become to Satan. Thus, the harder he works to bring us down."[4] That's why Jesus said we must constantly "keep watch and pray, so that you will not give in to temptation. For the spirit is willing, but the body is weak" (Mark 14:38, NLT).

Please read 1 Peter 5:8. Satan is determined to destroy God's people. And on our own, we are simply no match for Lucifer and his evil forces. When John wrote, "He who is in you is greater than he who is in the world" (1 John 4:4, NKJV), he was saying, by implication, that without Christ we are less powerful than the devil.

So what's to keep us from feeling outmatched, giving up, and jumping head-long into the depths of sin when temptation comes our way? Sigmund Freud would have us believe it is our "ego" (self-control) and "super-id" (conscience) that keep us in check. But no amount of determination, moral ethics, or societal pressures can help us "keep our dukes up" day in and day out. No, it's not the super-id that will help us overcome; it is the super*natural*, super*power* of Jesus.

The Weapons of Our Warfare

Please read Ephesians 6:14-17. When Paul described the "whole armor of God" needed "to stand against the wiles of the devil," every piece he listed is defensive except one. The one offensive weapon we have is the Word of God—the Spirit's sword can utterly annihilate the enemy. When we hide God's Word in our hearts and quote it aloud to our adversary during times of temptation, we will "not sin against [God]" (Psalm 119:11). More so, the *truth* of Scripture will force the powers of darkness to flee.

In 2 Chronicles 20 the "weapon" the children of Judah used as they marched toward their enemies was praise. Their praise was effective because it was based on the *truth* of God and his Scripture. Likewise, our biblical praise frustrates and confuses those imps of the dark world. Thus, the next time you're tempted to get discouraged or frightened or rebellious, turn your eyes upward toward heaven and Jesus. Praise him fervently and know that your invisible enemies are scurrying away in horror and defeat.

Notice that the people of Judah didn't lay down their weapons of worship once their enemies were slain. Rather, they continued to praise "with harps and lutes and trumpets" right into "the temple of the Lord" (2 Chronicles 20:28). The people of Judah kept on doing what they were supposed to do even after they had won their battle. That put them in a fine position to potentially and eventually *finish well*. If we have aspirations of finishing well, we, too, must keep on doing what we're supposed to do—for one, we must keep fighting the *good fight* of faith.

Part of Judah's joyful worship on the way back from victory no doubt included some fancy footwork. (When you're that happy, it's bound to affect your feet!) So if you are physically able, stand up and do a little dance of praise before the Lord. Your body will hate you for it, but your spirit will be reminded it's not about you and your flesh. It's about showing how much you love your Lord! Go ahead. You'll never be in the mood. Just make this sacrifice of praise anyway!

What inspires people to keep fighting even in the most formidable circumstances? What drives them? For Magallanes it was apparently his love for his fellow soldiers. For our precious Jesus, it was love for his Father and for humanity that drove him to Calvary. He fought Satan himself to buy back the deed to our souls. He accomplished his mission. He finished *well*.

What drives you to keep fighting and not give in? Only pure love for the Lord and others is an effective motivator in the long run. Have you submitted every area of yourself to God? If not, you cannot fight Satan and win. He will spear you directly through that place in your armor that you have left unprotected. Write your prayer of response below.

{ JOURNAL

Day 2: Keep Focused

Years after his death, Tommy Armour is still considered by many to be one of the greatest golf instructors ever. His book *How to Play Your Best Golf All the Time* is a must-read for serious golfers. In it, Armour reveals the secret to being the best golfer one can be. He writes, "It is not solely the capacity to make great shots that makes champions, but the essential quality of making very few bad shots."[5] Anyone has the capability to do something extraordinary at least once in a while. But real winners are those who remain attentive to their game and disciplined in their thoughts and actions. The path to victory demands their total concentration and devotion. They remain determined not to disqualify themselves through careless mistakes and poor judgment. In the long run, staying focused and staying consistent is the greater challenge.

The Apostle Paul was up to the challenge. He viewed his entire life as a race, a race he did not intend to lose. He wrote, "I discipline my body like an athlete, training it to do what it should. Otherwise, I fear that after preaching to others I myself might be disqualified" (1 Corinthians 9:27, NLT). Apparently his disciplinary techniques worked. Near the end of his life, he wrote to Timothy, "I have finished the race" (2 Timothy 4:7).

Please read 1 Corinthians 9:24-27. What motivated Paul to be self-controlled? What was Paul concerned might happen to him, and what was he doing to prevent it?

As we learned yesterday, Paul's mission in life was to influence as many as he could with the gospel of Christ. He knew what a devastating blow would be dealt to that mission if he were not to live out what he preached. Others who were once influenced by him would cast him away and ignore his message. Even harder for Paul to bear would be standing before his Savior and not hearing him say, "Well done." Obviously Paul was serious about finishing well. Nothing—not even his old nature—was going to stand in the way of him reaching his goal. Paul had his eyes on the prize.

Please read Paul's powerful resolve to remain focused in Philippians 3:12-14.

Have you ever watched the end of the World Series or the announcement of the gold-medal winner at an Olympic event? Even if I don't enjoy the sport, I love to see the athletes' reactions when they achieve their goals. It's exciting to see them have their moments as they jump up and down, hug their teammates, and shed tears. They've earned their celebration. They've been training and striving for it for years. Paul's "gold medal" was far greater than anything this earth has to offer. His was an incorruptible, heavenly prize, the "upward call of God in Christ" (NKJV).

Success to Significance

The people of Judah also had their eyes on a prize. But their prize wasn't quite as spiritual as Paul's; it was success against their enemies. As much as we might like to believe that every one of those choir members praised God purely out of great love for him, most likely some, if not several, were motivated more by a simple desire to live another day! Obedience to God wasn't only right and proper for them; it was *necessary* for their survival.

In the earlier stages of our Christian lives, our motivation for serving God is often for our own purposes. We have a ladder to climb and personal goals to reach. We are driven by success. I'm not saying that is necessarily bad. If by success we mean being all we can be for God's glory, then success is a wonderful goal. Having God's hand on our lives ensures that we develop into people God can use to the fullest extent on this earth. Nonetheless, personal gain, no matter how pure our motives, is just that—personal. At some point, we need to shift our focus from personal success to seeking *significance* and striving to make a lasting impact on our world and on others.

I don't believe it's too big a stretch to say that as the children of Judah collected the spoils during the days after the battle, they enjoyed a much-needed time of rest and refocusing. No longer was success their pressing goal; that pinnacle had been reached. Now they turned their attention to taking what the Lord had blessed them with and investing it in their families, children, nation, and Temple. They had a new and greater prize awaiting them. No wonder they returned with such joy to Jerusalem (2 Chronicles 20:27). They had accomplished their original mission; now they had revitalized and redefined vision, passion, and purpose. Wow, talk about revival!

A Few Things to Keep in Mind

I don't know about you, but a good infusion of renewed passion and purpose is exactly what I need sometimes. It's not terribly difficult to focus on a short-term ministry goal, such as preparing for a church musical or completing a Bible study. Most of us can pull off some level of consistency for a brief period. But let's face it: Having to be "up" day in and day out for those who count on our Christian example can be very challenging.

The writer of Hebrews gives us some important pointers that can help us keep focused for the long haul. 🐦 Please read Hebrews 12:1-2.

Distractions will take our attention off our goals. These act as weights that slow us down, discourage us, and even detour us. Satan has a whole bag of tricks designed to distract and ensnare us. One is to place in our paths activities that seem harmless or even helpful, but they are not the will of God for us. Notice also that we are to "throw off...the sin that so easily entangles," indicating that the distraction could be a specific habitual sin. That "hidden fault" (Psalm 19:12) of ours must go if we are to stay the course.

Discipline is required to keep us focused. In the story of the tortoise and the hare, the turtle was much slower than the rabbit, but the turtle set his pace and ultimately won the race. Anybody can have a great start, but seasoned runners know how to set a pace that will allow them to remain consistent and energized for the high hills and long stretches ahead. And while others are off having fun, they stay committed to finish well.

The *direction* of our focus is obviously imperative. (It helps to know which way we're supposed to go!) Our minds should be "on things above, not on earthly things" (Colossians 3:2). Seeing Jesus and becoming like him—that is our high calling, nothing more, nothing less. Chuck Swindoll puts it like this: "The very best thing for the minister to do is live a life of authenticity, accountability, and humility."[6]

Divine power is absolutely required for us to focus and finish well. In fact, as stated in this passage, we are not the "finisher" [from NKJV] of our faith; Jesus is. He started the salvation process in us, and he alone will complete it. One of my favorite verses is Philippians 1:6: "I am certain that God, who began the good work within you, will continue his work until it is finally finished on the day when Christ Jesus returns" (NLT).

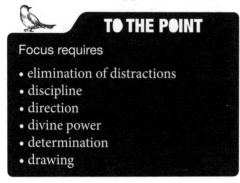

TO THE POINT

Focus requires

- elimination of distractions
- discipline
- direction
- divine power
- determination
- drawing

Determination is also needed to maintain focus along the way. As worshippers and worship leaders, every one of us should have a carefully crafted mission statement for our lives. It should be written and shared with someone who will help us stay accountable to it. We should set weekly goals that move us toward it. And we should willingly lay aside any activities or goals that don't fit into God's mission for us.

Drawn, Not Driven

At a recent retreat, John Corts, longtime chief operating officer of the Billy Graham Evangelistic Association, said something that caught my attention. He said, "Christians aren't meant to be driven. We are drawn." He went on to explain that what lies ahead for Christians should pull us toward heaven and our Savior. We should not have to be pushed and prodded every week. In fact, if we constantly need motivating and propping up just to get us to do what we're called to do, then we've lost sight of heaven's splendor. The men of Judah didn't need someone standing behind them urging them to return to Jerusalem from the battlefield. They went joyfully. And when they came into town, they didn't go first to their homes. They went straight to the Temple. They were *drawn* to it because their first priority and first love was their Lord.

No one has to tell a young man in love that he needs to call his girl and go see her. Likewise, when we fall head over heels in love with Jesus, no one should have to tell us to set our sights on him and talk to him every chance we get!

My Daily Praise

Clap your hands before the Lord and tell him *out loud* how awesome he is. Focus on his greatness and holiness. Praise him for his majesty. Don't be concerned about necessarily clapping in rhythm. Just clap with your hands and your heart lifted upward. "Clap your hands, all you peoples; shout to God with loud songs of joy" (Psalm 47:1, NRSV). Try singing or whistling a song while you clap your hands to the Lord.

How has your love life with the Lord been lately? How often do you talk to him and read his Word? When you sing or play praise songs, do you do it more out of habit and obligation, or do you look forward to every time you can love Jesus through your worship? What activities or thoughts compete for your attention and focus? Are you disciplining yourself to keep growing in your love for him and in the talents and opportunities he has given you? Write your prayer of response below.

JOURNAL

Day 3: Keep Faithful

A few days before my 40th birthday, I received an e-mail promoting a large worship conference at Saddleback Church in California. Some of the most well-known worship leaders and bands were to be a part of it. As I sat looking at the photos on the promotional literature, I couldn't help but wonder, "Am I where I am today because this is God's perfect will for me, or could it be that God couldn't elevate me to the next level of influence because he couldn't trust me? Is the only difference between the people on the poster and me a matter of calling and talent? Or could it be that their hearts are more pure, their hunger to know God more intense, and their walk with God more consistent?"

I sensed at that moment that God wanted to place me in an arena of greater influence during the second half of my life. I had no doubt that my most significant impact was yet to come. However, for that to happen, I knew that all sin and selfish motives and ways must be eradicated from my life. I must be *trustworthy*.

In 1 Timothy 1:12, Paul wrote, "And I thank Christ Jesus our Lord, who hath enabled me, for that he counted me faithful, putting me into the ministry" (KJV). The New Living Translation puts it like this: "I thank Christ Jesus our Lord, who has given me strength to do his work. He considered me trustworthy and appointed me to serve him."

Paul was appointed to the ministry because God could trust him. Obviously, God takes our faithfulness—or *lack* of faith—very seriously.

🕊 Please read Matthew 24:45-51. Jesus describes what the master will do for the servant he finds carrying out his orders and what he will do to the one he finds disobeying his orders. Jesus reiterates this profound principle of cause and effect, faithfulness vs. unfaithfulness in the very next chapter (see Matthew 25:14-30).

We are being faithful to God when we do what he tells us to do. When we consistently and willingly obey him without hesitation, he knows we can be relied upon. The children of Judah proved themselves to be reliable. God instructed them through his prophet Jahaziel to take up their positions against their enemies and then "stand firm and see the deliverance the Lord will give you" (2 Chronicles 20:17). Unlike many of us who want to question God's wisdom or suggest another plan in moments like this, Jehoshaphat and the people of Judah joyfully and immediately embraced his orders. God rewarded their faithfulness with a great victory beyond what anyone could have imagined. Here we see the principle of cause and effect that Jesus talked about: They were obedient in how they defeated a few enemies; by the time they returned home, God had caused them to be feared among *many* enemies. The result of their simple obedience was peace all around them (2 Chronicles 20:29-30).

Faithful to the Finish

It is one thing to be faithful though a particular crisis or period of our lives. It's quite another to stay faithful to the *end* of our lives. Israel had some shining moments in which the people clung to God and obeyed him completely. Yet, when we step back and view their entire history, we see that they consistently rebelled and became increasingly unfaithful to the Lord.

As we discovered yesterday, the life of a Christian is a race. However, running is not the same as winning. We can run an entire marathon, but if we quit just shy of the finish line we can't say we've truly finished. The same is true of remaining faithful to the end.

Paul did win. In 2 Timothy 4:7b he wrote, "I have remained faithful" (NLT); "I have kept the faith" (NKJV); "I have guarded the faith" (Weymouth New Testament); "I've...believed all the way" (*The Message*).

Throughout the centuries people have believed "all the way" to their final breath. Following are a few examples from *The New Foxe's Book of Martyrs*. Let me warn you that some of these are difficult to read. I encourage you to check out this amazing book if you'd like to learn about more Christians who finished faithfully and finished *well*.

Ignatius was the overseer of the church in Antioch. Because he professed Christ, he was sent to Rome. He wrote to the church in Rome, urging them not to try to deliver him from martyrdom because they would deprive him of that which he most longed and hoped for. "I care for nothing of visible or invisible things so that I may but win Christ. Let fire and the cross, let the companies of wild beasts, let breaking of bones and tearing of limbs, let the grinding of the whole body, and all the malice of the devil, come upon me; be it so, only may I win Christ Jesus." Even when he was sentenced to be thrown to wild beasts and could hear them roaring, he so desired to suffer for Christ that he said, "I am the wheat of Christ: I am going to be ground with the teeth of wild beasts, that I may be found pure bread."[7]

Under the persecutions of Roman Emperor Marcus Aurelius, some Christian martyrs had their feet crushed in presses and were forced to walk over sharp, pointed objects. Then they were killed in terrible ways. Yet few turned from Christ or even asked those who tortured them to alleviate their suffering.[8]

Just a few years ago at a Bible camp in Indonesia, 15-year-old Roy Pontoh was threatened with death by an angry mob. Even though he was terrified, he would not renounce his faith in Jesus Christ. When they told him that he must become a Muslim, the boy quavered, "I am a soldier of Christ." An enraged Muslim ripped the boy's stomach open with a knife. Just before he died, Roy said one final word: "Jesus."[9]

In 1981 a Dutch couple was about to return to Afghanistan, where they had been missionaries. The country had been taken over by Communists, and the couple knew they were returning to an environment hostile to Jesus Christ. Asked if they were afraid to return, they replied, "We know only one great danger—not to be in the center of God's will." Not long afterward, they were cut to pieces. At their gravesides, their 5-year-old son said, "I forgive the men who killed my mother and father."[10]

Jesus said, "If you remain faithful even when facing death, I will give you the crown of life" (Revelation 2:10b, NLT). The people we just read about most certainly received a crown of life, for they remained faithful to the end.

Missing the Mark

Not every person described in *The New Foxe's Book of Martyrs* had such a happy ending. Some, in fact, chose to recant their faith and renounce Christ rather than suffer for him. They *didn't* finish so well. Neither did Moses, David, King Asa, and a few other notables from the Bible. They had great starts, but somewhere along the way they stumbled. Even Jehoshaphat, the star of our anchor story, made a serious error in judgment toward the end of his life. The last detail we read of him was his entering into an unholy alliance with the wicked king of Israel. (See 2 Chronicles 20:35-37.)

It's sadly interesting to note that all these men of the Old Testament were in their "second half," that season of life when they had the greatest opportunity to have a positive impact on others and leave a great legacy. Unfaithfulness can sneak up on us at any age, no matter how long we've been Christians.

Read 2 Peter 1:3-9. We must realize that we have "everything we need for life and godliness" through knowing Jesus and having his promises fulfilled in our lives. We have no excuse not to live faithful lives. But if we're not careful, we can become "ineffective and unproductive" in our walk (verse 8). It's happened to others; it can happen to you and me.

On that early morning three days before my 40th birthday, I pondered whether God could really trust me. Here is the prayer I wrote in my journal: "Oh God, create in me a pure heart. Renew a steadfast spirit within me. Help me no longer rest on my accomplishments of the past but strain toward what is ahead, pressing toward the mark for the prize of your high calling in Christ Jesus. May I not settle for mediocrity and comfort. Rather, may I run in such a way as to obtain the prize, beating my body, bringing it into subjection. Lord, as your eyes search to and fro across the earth, may you see and strongly support me because my heart is always and fully yours."

My Daily Praise

Today's study has been much more solemn (if not downright depressing!) than the others. God wants our praise to be authentic. Respond appropriately with your praise right now. I'm not referring to your mood but rather to the cry of your heart at this very moment. Perhaps kneeling and singing an intimate worship song to God would best express your love to your Savior now. Frankly, you may feel you need to confess a sinful attitude or action before you can do any authentic worshipping. Please do what God is leading you to do.

My Daily Surrender

Jim Elliot wrote, "He is no fool who gives what he cannot keep to gain what he cannot lose."[11] Jim Elliot and the martyrs we read about today were ordinary people like us who at the end of their lives were given the extraordinary grace to be able to die for God. We are not all called to be martyrs for Christ, but we are all commissioned to live every day in faithful obedience, joy, and devotion to him who loved us first and most.

Write a prayer of surrender to God's perfect will; then thank him for where he has placed you at this moment in your life.

JOURNAL }

Day 4: Keep Fresh

If you are like most everyone else on the planet, you don't like stale food. We enjoy and prefer things that are fresh. (There's a reason a "Hot Doughnuts Now" sign makes our mouths water.) In much the same way, God enjoys people who are fresh, Christians who still have the joy of the Lord and a passion to know him more, regardless of their age. These are the ones who represent him best because they demonstrate the fresh life he has given them.

Motion pictures were created to amuse people and help them escape their own realities for a while. For about two hours, movies launch us into a fantasy world of excitement, intrigue, romance, or adventure. We transcend the normal and mundane. Unfortunately for some, when "The End" appears on the screen, they are forced back into the real world, to lives that are usually anything but thrilling and adventurous. For some, the problems, pressures, and routines of daily life eventually turn them sour and stale.

This shouldn't be the case for the Christian. When we consider movie stars, our first thought shouldn't be to envy them. If they don't have Christ at the center of their souls, they don't have true life at all. They're just existing, grabbing at pleasure and purpose here and there as best they can. If anything, they should envy *us!* We have the Creator of the universe and the overcomer of death living inside us. Life should be *bursting* out of a Christian. In fact, Jesus said, "I am come that they might have life, and that they might have it more abundantly" (John 10:10b, KJV).

Talk about having a reason to be envied: What the children of Judah experienced in 2 Chronicles 20 had the makings of a Hollywood action movie! The climactic moment in their action film came when they peered into the valley where all their enemies lay lifeless before them. The resolution of this story's plot was their collecting of the spoils. This bigger-than-life drama even has a happy ending, complete with joyful songs of praise to make everyone smile. It was the perfect time to "roll the credits" as they gathered to celebrate the miraculous destruction of their enemies.

But then that was it. The "show" was over. Now it was time for them to come away from the "theater" of victory and return to the normal, everyday activities of life. "All the men of Judah and Jerusalem returned joyfully to Jerusalem, for the Lord had given them cause to rejoice" (2 Chronicles 20:27). The amazing thing is that they were *still* joyful and enthusiastic even after they got home! To finish well, as Judah's army did, we, too, must return week after week to our places of ministry still joyful, still consistently enthusiastic because the Lord has given us "cause to rejoice."

Paul's Example

Please turn to 2 Timothy 4 now and begin reading Paul's final words to Timothy in verse 8. What did Paul say in this verse that might cause you to believe his faith in the Lord was still very much alive and fresh?

What tipped me off to Paul's fresh faith was what he said at the end of verse 8: "not only to me, but also to all who have longed for his appearing." Understand that Paul wasn't sitting in a plush hotel, eating fruits and berries while servants catered to his every whim. Paul was in a cold, dark cell with chains on his feet and his hands. (See 2 Timothy 2:9 and 4:13.) He was facing certain death. Many people under such circumstances would have blamed, even cursed God. But shackles and chains couldn't prevent Paul's heart from jumping with joy as he yearned for his Lord's return. Although his body was wasting away, his spirit was "being renewed every day" (2 Corinthians 4:16, NLT).

Staying Fresh and Green

So how do we remain fresh from week to week and year to year? How can we be constantly renewed, as Paul was?

Please read Psalm 92:12-15. Try to identify three ingredients that are necessary for us to flourish and stay fresh and growing even in our "old age."

First, we need to *stay planted in God's Word*. Strong trees must be firmly rooted in good soil. Psalm 1:2-3 says that those who continually delight and meditate on "the law of the Lord" will be "like a tree planted by the rivers of water, that brings forth its fruit in its season, whose leaf also shall not wither; and whatever he does shall prosper"(NKJV).

The second necessary element to keep fresh and green is to *stay prayerful in God's presence*, basking in his perfect light. We must cultivate a life of continual prayer, praise, and dependence on our Father. "Pray without ceasing," as 1 Thessalonians 5:17 [NKJV] tells us. We should never get used to coming before God. German theologian Rudolf Otto contends that the end of true worship is a sense of "mystical awe" in the presence of God.[12] When we feel we no longer need to bow to his holiness and power, our hearts have already become old, cold, and crusty.

Finally, we must *stay pure in God's holiness*, free from outside pollutants. If God does not dabble in sin, neither should we. Sin slowly but effectively poisons our sensitivity to the Holy Spirit and steals our joy and innocence.

Forever Young

Choosing to live in "the courts of the Lord" is wonderfully freeing and downright fun at times. "A happy heart is like good medicine" (Proverbs 17:22a, NCV). And when we have God's peace and joy in our hearts, laughter comes easily. My mom has managed to stay young at heart into her 70s. In fact she was a youth director at 71. She built a large youth group on nothing but the grace of God, her contagious spirit, and the hot biscuits she served every Sunday night!

When Paul wrote his final letter to Timothy, he was in his late 60s. He stayed fresh and on fire for the Lord even into his twilight years.

When I was 12, an evangelist named Clayton Shaw came to our church. He was in his mid-60s at the time. I was mesmerized by his passion and excitement. One night during the revival, the men invited me to pray with them. Right in the middle of our prayer time, Clayton started singing "Amazing Grace." As he sang, he lifted his hands in praise, and tears flowed down his cheeks. Over the years I had several opportunities to work with this great saint, and every time without exception he was full of joy and love for his Savior and for the lost. Clayton kept fresh right up to his homecoming day, and many lives were touched and changed because of it.

Psalm 103:5 tells us that God longs to "satisfy" the desires of his children "with good things" and to renew our youth "like the eagle's." It is his will for us to remain fresh and relevant as we represent him to each generation. He can show us his ways

TO THE POINT

How to Stay Fresh and Green
• stay planted in God's Word
• stay prayerful in God's presence
• stay pure in God's holiness

if we are not so set in our own ways. He will soften our old hearts and give us new hearts if we will simply choose to live *daily* in his courts of praise.

My Daily Praise

According to Psalm 92:14-15, one of the ways we can tell if a Christian is "fresh and green" is his proclamation of God's praise. In Psalm 71, the psalmist writes, "For you have been my hope, O Sovereign Lord, my confidence since my youth" (verse 5). Later he writes, "As for me, I will always have hope; I will praise you more and more" (verse 14). God had been and always would be the psalmist's hope. The older he got the more determined he was to praise his Lord. Write a prayer thanking God for helping you praise him "more and more."

JOURNAL

Ben Franklin once quipped, "Life's tragedy is that we get old too soon and wise too late." Perhaps God has shone his light on your soul and exposed it as old and stale. Perhaps he's not as precious and sweet to you today as he was last week or last year. Ask him to make you fresh and green in his presence once again.

JOURNAL }

Day 5: Keep Fruitful

We need to learn one more principle from our anchor story in 2 Chronicles 20. Jehoshaphat, the musicians, and the victorious army returned to Jerusalem, worshipping their Deliverer at the top of their lungs. Then "the fear of God came upon all the kingdoms of the countries when they heard how the Lord had fought against the enemies of Israel" (verse 29). The profound truth that we cannot miss is the impact their trust in the Lord and their obedience to him had on everyone around them.

Before we reach the bottom of our metaphorical mountain and finish our journey, think about something: Who first told you about Jesus? Who on earth more than anyone else helped you to trust him as your Savior? Since you've become a Christian, who has taken the most time and shown the most interest in helping you grow in your faith?

If you and I are strong, healthy Christians today, chances are good it is because somebody deliberately invested his or her self in us by teaching us about the Lord and about following him.

Stop and thank God for those individuals who have loved you enough to point you toward heaven and help you grow in your walk with God.

Psalm 92:14 describes one more significant and consistent characteristic of Christians who are fresh and green: "They will still bear fruit in old age." They are still refreshing those around them and reproducing themselves by leading others to know their God as they do.

Please read 2 Timothy 1:2. Paul had no blood relation to Timothy that we know of. So why do you think Paul called Timothy his son? Paul had invested many hours over the years teaching and nurturing Timothy in the faith. He may even have led Timothy to the Lord during his first visit to Lystra. In essence, Paul had reproduced himself spiritually through Timothy. It was therefore appropriate for him to refer to Timothy as his son. Furthermore, Paul called Timothy his "dear son." He had grown close to Timothy and loved him deeply. Even near the end of his life, Paul was pouring himself into Timothy, sharing his knowledge and experience so that Timothy would "be strong in the grace that is in Christ Jesus" (2 Timothy 2:1).

Modern-Day Mentors

People are still pouring their lives into helping others grow and become the strong men and women God intended them to be. One shining example is S. Truett Cathy, founder of Chick-fil-A restaurants. In his book *Eat Mor Chikin: Inspire More People*, Cathy writes, "The restaurant business gives us a wonderful opportunity to mentor young people and help guide them toward adulthood."[13] One of my favorite stories he shares is about a young boy named Woody Faulk.

Listen to how Cathy tells it:

"Woody's parents had divorced when he was four years old… He was on a Scout trip when word came to him that his mother had been killed in an automobile accident. His grandparents were dead, and his father had not been in contact for years, so Woody was sent to live with an aunt and uncle in…Atlanta. They brought him to my Sunday school class, and I soon became aware of his situation. I immediately noticed his high standards and capabilities…He visited Jeannette and me at the farm several times, and I asked him at one point to let me see his report card. He said later that I was the first man ever to ask him about his schoolwork. Knowing someone was genuinely interested, he made straight A's from that point on. Jeannette and I grew to love Woody… He became like an adopted child to us…When Woody graduated, I told him I hoped that he would come to work with Chick-fil-A…He is now Vice President, Brand Development. When Woody and his wife, Rae, married, he asked me to serve as his best man…"[14]

Cathy went from being a perfect stranger to this young guy to being the best man at his wedding! That is exactly what can happen when we simply make time—and *take* time—to invest the experiences and understanding God has given us in another person.

Jesus' Plan to Reach the World

No one has set a better example of one-on-one mentoring than Jesus himself. Think about how Jesus prioritized his time while he was on earth. He knew he had only about three years to have an impact on this world. Yet he invested the majority of his precious time with just 12 men! He handpicked these disciples and instructed them every day. They got to see his attitudes, his methods, his reactions to difficult situations. When they got off track, he was right there beside them to correct them and redirect them.

Jesus invested his last hours on this earth not with huge masses of people, but rather with his 11 disciples. These were the ones he knew he could trust to finish his work of reaching the world. He had reproduced and multiplied himself through these men. And they went out and multiplied themselves. Then the disciples' disciples went out and made even more disciples. Thus the gospel of Jesus Christ spread throughout the entire known world in a matter of years!

This is exactly what Paul was explaining to Timothy in his last letter.

Please read 2 Timothy 2:2. Paul wanted to be sure Timothy grasped this simple but profound plan of multiplication, God's blueprint to build a "spiritual house" of Chrisians down through the generations. (See 1 Peter 2:5.)

I am unspeakably thankful for the small discipleship groups I was involved with in college. I am indebted to the leaders of those groups who invested in me to sharpen and challenge me. I realized then where I would make my greatest impact and leave my most lasting legacy. It would not be enough for me to sing in large arenas or teach masses of people. My most significant ministry would be through those individuals God leads across my path, those along life's journey in which I invest personal and individual time and resources—people who, in turn, disciple others.

No Time to Waste

Our time on this earth is very short. That is why David prayed, "Teach us to count our days that we may gain a wise heart" (Psalm 90:12, NRSV).

Please read Psalm 90. David gives us a formula for "counting our days" in verse 4.

One night a few years ago I was lying awake when a thought hit me: If a thousands years is like a 12-hour day to God (a "watch in the night"), then how long is the average human life span to God? The question intrigued me so much that I had to go find a calculator. What I discovered astounded me.

The average life expectancy of a person is about 75 years. But to God, that is only 54 minutes. That's less than an hour. That's less time than it takes some people to drive to work or mow their lawn or sit though an English class. Talk about humbling and eye-opening.

Give it a try. Multiply your age by 0.72 to find out how many *minutes* old you are in God's eyes.

It's no wonder that the psalmist went on to write that we are "like the new grass of the morning…though in the morning it springs up new, by evening it is dry and withered" (verses 5-6). Our lives are short. We don't have time to live outside God's will. We don't have one minute to waste if we are to finish well.

My Daily Praise

Congratulations! We've made it to the bottom of the mountain!

Now as we stand here in the valley, join me and "lift up your eyes to the fields." Do you see that they are ripe with people who need to know that our God lives and he loves them enough to die? (See John 4:35.) They need to see genuine worship and passionate praise flowing from our lives every day.

Praise God out loud right now. Thank him for opening your eyes to see more clearly what he wants you to do. Don't stop this praise time until your heart has deliberately and joyfully given God the praise that is due to him. He is unfathomably worthy!

My Daily Surrender

Until we willingly apply the cross to our lives by dying daily to ourselves, we will never praise him more powerfully, and we cannot possibly finish well. Jesus never lost focus of the cross. He calls to us to do the same: "If anyone desires to come after Me, let him deny himself, and take up his cross, and follow Me" (Matthew 16:24, NKJV).

God has shown us some profound and life-changing things during this study. And "to whom much is given, from him much will be required" (Luke 12:48, NKJV). So we are now *required* to live out what we have learned and to tell what we have experienced—through praise that is more *pure* and more *powerful*.

Write out a prayer surrendering the rest of your life to God now.

JOURNAL

1. The HighRoad.org, "Wounded Marine keeps fighting" (http://www.thehighroad.org/showthread.php?t=132123).
2. Alfred Plummer, *The Pastoral Epistles* (New York: A.C. Armstrong and Son, 1903), 348.
3. John MacArthur, *The MacArthur Study Bible* (Nashville, TN: Word Publishing, 1997), 1871.
4. Charles Stanley, *Winning the War Within* (Nashville, TN: Thomas Nelson Publishers, 1988), 163.
5. Tommy Armour, *How to Play Your Best Golf All the Time* (New York: Simon and Schuster, 1953), 12.
6. Charles R. Swindoll, *Hope Again* (Dallas, TX: Word Publishing, 1996), 229.
7. John Foxe, *The New Foxe's Book of Martyrs* (Gainesville, FL: Bridge-Logos Publishers, 2001), 14.
8. Ibid., 16.
9. Ibid., 376-377.
10. Ibid., 340.
11. Elisabeth Elliot, *Shadow of the Almighty* (San Francisco: Harper & Row, 1979), 15.
12. Douglas Banister, *The Word and Power Church* (Grand Rapids, MI: Zondervan Publishing House, 1999), 149.
13. S. Truett Cathy, *Eat Mor Chikin: Inspire More People* (Decatur, GA: Looking Glass Books, 2002), 48.
14. Ibid., 129-130.

GROUP SESSIONS

INTRODUCTION

These group sessions will provide a forum for the members of your worship team to share their insights from the previous week's readings. But they serve an even more important purpose: By engaging in a simple but compelling experience linked to each week's lesson, participants will learn a significant truth about praise and worship. In short, they'll be much more likely to remember and apply the truths they've read about during the week.

Each experience is simple, requires no preparation, and takes no more than 15 minutes. Some experiences are fun; some are somber; all are thought-provoking. In addition, they will bring the members of your group together in meaningful conversation and, over the course of this nine-week study, will deepen their relationships.

In fact, the more participants share their personal stories and discoveries each week, the more they will become a genuine team, working together and worshipping together—a reflection of the healthy body of Christ.

I encourage you to spend a few minutes each week reading and familiarizing yourself with the session so you can lead it in a natural, spontaneous way. I'm confident that you'll enjoy these times with your worship team and that they'll lead to unforgettable moments!

WEEK 1: Understanding Worship
Theme: Every aspect of our lives can be an act of worship.
Supplies: A watch or clock with a second hand
Preparation: None

After all the members of your team have arrived and had time to settle, lead them in this simple experience. First ask the team to form trios. Then explain that two people in each trio will stand on either side of the other member of the trio. As the two people firmly hold the arms of the person in the middle against his or her sides, that person will try to raise his or her arms. After about 30 seconds of unyielding pressure, have the two people on either side release the person's arms and step away. As the pressure is lifted, the arms of the person in the middle will rise of their own volition.

Have trio members take turns standing in the middle so that everyone experiences this phenomenon. After everyone has participated, call the entire group together and lead them in debriefing the experience. (If there are more than 12 people on your team, have them discuss their responses in pairs or trios.) Say:

Let's talk about this experience.

- What sensations did you feel as you tried and failed to raise your arms?

- What about when the pressure was lifted—how did your body react?

- How did that feel, emotionally?

This week we explored the nature of worship. A key to wholehearted worship is the willingness to submit to God and acknowledge his sovereignty in our lives.

- How have you struggled to release control of your life and hand it over to God?

- How is that effort similar to this experience? How is it different?

- How has the desire to control events and people affected your ability to worship?

Close in prayer, asking God to help you and your team experience the freedom and joy that come from allowing God to take his proper place at the center of your lives.

WEEK 2: Understanding Praise
Theme: We were designed to praise God.
Supplies: None
Preparation: None

After your team has arrived, and everyone has had a chance to greet one an-other, get everyone's attention and ask them to participate in a simple exercise. Ask them to clasp their hands together as if in prayer. After they've done this, ask them to notice which thumb is on top. Then ask them to clasp their hands together again, this time making sure the opposite thumb is on top.

Ask everyone to turn to a partner and quickly discuss their responses to these questions:

- **How did it feel to clasp your hands differently than you normally do?**
- **How was this like or unlike changing the outward expression of your worship?**

This week we've been exploring the idea that we—and all of creation—were designed to praise God. But over time, we've all gotten used to praising God in certain ways. We've gotten so used to those ways, in fact, that other expressions of worship may seem unnatural to us. But, just as it's perfectly natural to clasp our hands in an unaccustomed way, it's also natural to praise God in new ways.

Close in prayer, asking God to help you and your team discover new and exciting ways to worship him, even if that means moving outside of your comfort zones.

WEEK 3: The God We Worship
Theme: The more we know of God, the greater our worship of him will be.
Supplies: A watch or clock with a second hand
Preparation: None

After everyone has arrived, get the group's attention and invite everyone to take part in a quick, fun activity. Tell them that they'll all have one minute to greet five people individually. Here's the catch: They must not speak, and they must find a new way to make contact with each person. So for example, if they shake hands with the first person, they must find a different way to silently greet the second, third, and so on. This should lead to lots of laughter and funny antics!

After a minute has elapsed, ask participants to each find a partner and discuss their responses to these questions:

- **How easy or hard was it to find new ways to greet people?**

- **What benefits can come from finding new ways to do a routine thing? What are some drawbacks?**

- **What about your approach to worship? In what ways has it become routine?**

- **What can you do to reignite the passion and awe that accompanies genuine worship?**

After pairs have had sufficient time to discuss these questions, call the group back together. Ask several volunteers to share the fruits of their discussions. Then say:

As Dwayne Moore points out in this week's readings, it's easy to get stuck in a rut when we think of God. We tend to acknowledge only those attributes we can comprehend. As a result, the genuine reverence and awe we should feel for God can be reduced to mere ritual and obligation. Before you leave, think of at least one thing you can do this week to deepen your understanding of God. It's exciting to think of how our ever-deepening relationships with God will be reflected in our praise and worship in the upcoming weeks!

WEEK 4: Hearing God's Voice
Theme: To know God, we must learn to listen for his voice.
Supplies: A watch or clock, paper, and pencils or pens
Preparation: None

After the group has arrived, give everyone a sheet of paper and a pen or pencil. Tell them you'd like them to leave the room and find a place indoors or outdoors where they can be alone. (If your group is too large to disperse, simply ask people to sit quietly where they are.) Explain that for the next five minutes they are to simply listen and write down every sound they hear.

After five minutes, call the group back together and lead them through a debriefing. Ask:

- **What surprised you about this experience?**
- **What sounds did you notice for the first time?**
- **What sounds were especially prevalent?**
- **What would it mean to listen this intensely when you're trying to hear from God?**
- **What do you need to do to fine-tune your hearing so you don't miss God's "still small voice"?**

To conclude this experience, ask everyone to be quiet for about 30 seconds and listen carefully for what God may be saying to them. Close with a prayer of response.

WEEK 5: Five Essentials of Effective Worship Services
Theme: For our worship to be powerful, we must welcome both God's leading and that of our pastors.
Supplies: A watch or clock
Preparation: None

After everyone has arrived, begin rehearsing the upcoming week's music. About halfway through the rehearsal, stop abruptly and ask everyone to "take five." Explain that you'd like them, if possible, to scatter to different parts of the room or the facility, sit or lie down, close their eyes, and spend five minutes in quiet rest.

After five minutes, call the group back together, and lead them through a debriefing. Ask:

- **How did you react initially when I interrupted our rehearsal?**
- **How did your perspective change during five minutes of rest?**

Find a partner and talk about a time God used an interruption to get your attention, remind you of his presence, or bless you in some other way.

At the conclusion of the discussion, lead the group in prayer, asking God to help you all recognize his leading in every aspect of your lives, even interruptions that derail your plans.

WEEK 6: Qualities of Leadership
Theme: We are called to serve others.
Supplies: A watch or clock with a second hand
Preparation: None

After everyone has arrived, explain that you'd like the group to take part in an experience that will reveal something about themselves as well as our culture.

Ask participants to form groups of three or four and then stand in a circle with their groups. Explain that when you say "go," the person in each foursome wearing the most blue will have one minute to describe a time he or she served someone else. The catch is that the speaker may not use the word *I*. Rather, that person must refer to himself or herself in the third person.

After a minute has elapsed, get everyone's attention, and ask the people standing to the right of the first speakers to repeat the exercise. Continue to do this until everyone has participated.

Call the group back together, and ask them to share their responses to these questions:

- **What did this experience reveal to you about serving?**
- **What are possible consequences of removing the word I from your mind and your speech in your role as a worship leader?**

Conclude by challenging everyone to find at least one way to serve someone at church, at home, or in the community in a fresh, unexpected way during the upcoming week. Then close with a prayer asking God to give you all a servant's heart.

WEEK 7: Using Our Tools Wisely
Theme: We are called to embrace worship music that accurately describes God, regardless of our own musical preferences.
Supplies: Paper and pens or pencils
Preparation: None

After your group has gathered, give everyone a sheet of paper and a pen or pencil. Ask them to sign their names as they normally do. Then ask them to sign their names using their nondominant hands. (So those who are left-handed will use their right hands and vice versa.) Ask:

- **What sensations and emotions did this exercise evoke?**

Now ask everyone to sign their names with their nondominant hands eight or nine more times. After they've done this, ask:

- **By the time you'd done this several times, how did your feelings differ from the first time you tried it?**
- **When have you encountered new ways of worshipping God that at first didn't feel right? How did you react? How did you overcome resistance to the new ways?**

Conclude this experience by asking everyone to stand in a circle and hold hands. Pray, asking God to open the hearts and minds of everyone there to different and creative ways to praise him, even if those ways cause them to feel uncomfortable or awkward at first.

WEEK 8: Five Goals for Lead Worshippers
Theme: The primary goal of worship leaders is to point others toward God.
Supplies: None
Preparation: None

After everyone has arrived, tell them you'd like them to stay for about five minutes after rehearsal. Then, when the rehearsal is over, ask the group to form a circle. (If your group has more than 12 members, ask participants to form groups of four or five and gather in several circles.) Be sure to do this in a space that is big enough to allow the circle (or circles) to expand. Say:

> **Please put your arms around the waists of the people standing next to you. I'm going to read our closing devotional thought. Please enter into this experience in a spirit of prayer. Ready?**
>
> **Leading others in worship is an awesome privilege and responsibility. And we love to do it, or we wouldn't be here. But so many things can taint our hearts and, in turn, our praise.**
>
> **Sometimes we do or say things that separate us from others, and we can't fully enjoy the love God intends for us. If you've ever treated others in an un-Christ-like way, I'd like you to drop your arms to your sides.** (Pause.)
>
> **Sometimes we're more interested in what's comfortable and easy than in what's best for the people we lead in worship. If you've ever forgotten what's really best for other worshippers, take a step backward.** (Pause.)
>
> **Sometimes we don't feel worshipful at all. If you've ever tried to lead worship when your heart was apathetic, take another step backward.** (Pause.)
>
> **Sometimes we turn away from people who could really use our encouragement. If you've ever ignored the needs of someone God has placed in your path, turn and face away from the center of the circle.** (Pause.)
>
> **Sometimes we become so self-absorbed that we forget to focus on God. If you've ever taken your eyes off of God and tried to depend solely on your own resources, close your eyes and keep them closed.** (Pause.)
>
> **As Christians, we're meant to love God and the people he has placed in our lives, but we're flawed human beings, and the truth is, we fail as often as we succeed.** (Pause.)
>
> **We build one another up and honor God when we encourage one another. If you've ever taken the time to speak a word of praise or encouragement to someone in the church or on our worship team, I'd like you to turn around.** (Pause.)

We reflect the heart of a servant when we bow to the preferences of others. If you've ever used a style of worship that was uncomfortable or difficult for you but served the needs of others, take one step forward. (Pause.)

We submit to God's authority when we recognize his sovereignty. If you've ever gratefully accepted God's will for your life, open your eyes. (Pause.)

We glorify God and inspire others when we worship God enthusiastically and passionately. If you've ever worshipped God with all that is within you, take another step forward. (Pause.)

God asks us to reach out in love to others. If you've ever reached out in Christian love, place your arms around the friends beside you—and say with me "amen!"

WEEK 9: Five Keys to Finishing Well
Theme: As long as we remain focused on God, our worship will be powerful and pure.
Supplies: None
Preparation: None

After everyone has arrived, ask them to take part in this simple exercise. Tell them to hold their arms straight out in front of them at shoulder level. Have them create a triangle by touching their index fingers together and their thumbs together. Then ask them to center this triangle on an object, such as a wall clock, that is at least 30 feet away. As soon as they've centered the object in the triangle, ask them to close their right eye. Then ask them to open both eyes, refocus on the object in the triangle, and close their left eye.

People will probably want to do this several times. When they've settled down, say:

> **This exercise tells you which eye is dominant. If the object remained in the center of the triangle when your right eye was closed, this means your left eye is dominant. If it remained in the center of the triangle when your left eye was closed, this means your right eye is dominant.**
>
> **In the same way, when we insist on being the dominant force in our lives, we lose sight of the prize: loving God and loving others. But when we allow God to dominate our hearts and minds, we never lose sight of that prize, and our lives and our worship reflect the wonder and glory of our God.**

Now ask participants to form groups of two or three to discuss their responses to the following questions. Ask:

- **In life, what causes you to take your focus off of God's perfect plan for you?**
- **In your role as a worship leader, what causes you to take your focus off of glorifying God and inspiring others through your worship?**

Close in prayer, asking God to help you and your team allow him to be the dominant force in your lives.

DEDICATION

To my family and to those 100 people who encouraged me as I wrote and journeyed with me as we made the first climb up this amazing mountain of discovery.

ACKNOWLEDGMENTS

My holy and awesome master, friend, and God for patiently instilling in me over 30 years the principles that are now in this book and for allowing me the privilege of passing them on to others. • My amazing and supportive wife, Sonia, and my boys, Stephen and Justin, for your patience and encouragement as I invested so many hours and days away from home to write. • Olda Phillips for the seed funds to begin the arduous search for a publisher. • Ken Galyean for being my prayer partner and encouraging me to write this book. • Brindlee Mountain Church for allowing me to hide away for 1,100 hours over two years to write while I was part of your staff. • The praise team at Brindlee Mountain Church for your invaluable comments and attentive ears as I taught you these principles before I wrote about them. • Cheryl Good for walking up to me that fateful day after our praise team devotional and saying, "Dwayne, you should write this stuff down." • My close friend Dr. Scott Dawson for connecting me with our mutual agent, David Sanford. • Dr. Terry Hadaway for lending your writing and editing expertise to my initial chapters. • My incredible literary agent, David Sanford, for never faltering in your belief in this book and for your guidance and confidence through the entire publishing process. • Rebekah Clark of Sanford Communications, Inc. for your untiring efforts to help find a publisher. • Elizabeth Jones of Sanford Communications for masterfully reshaping the interactive sections to make this a study for the masses. • Charles Billingsley for writing an amazing foreword. You really should write a book of your own some day! • John Martin, not only for being my dear friend and ministry partner, but also for having as much passion for this study and its potential as I do. • The Church at Ross Station and my pastor, Randy Norris, for your much-needed support and prayers as we worked to see this project over the finish line. • My many spiritual mentors as I was growing up—especially my mom—for consistently demonstrating before me godly and pure praise.